John Donne

Selected Poems

Edited by Richard Gill

Oxford University Press

OXFORD
UNIVERSITY PRESS

Great Clarendon Street, Oxford OX2 6DP

Oxford University Press is a department of the University of Oxford.
It furthers the University's objective of excellence in research, scholarship,
and education by publishing worldwide in

Oxford   New York

Auckland   Cape Town   Dar es Salaam   Hong Kong   Karachi
Kuala Lumpur   Madrid   Melbourne   Mexico City   Nairobi
New Delhi   Shanghai   Taipei   Toronto

With offices in

Argentina   Austria   Brazil   Chile   Czech Republic   France   Greece
Guatemala   Hungary   Italy   Japan   Poland   Portugal   Singapore
South Korea   Switzerland   Thailand   Turkey   Ukraine   Vietnam

Oxford is a registered trade mark of Oxford University Press
in the UK and in certain other countries.

ISBN-13: 978-0-19-831950-4
ISBN-10: 0-19-831950-9

Typeset by Koford Prints (Singapore) Ptd.Ltd.
Song Lin Building #06-02
No. 1 Syed Alwi Road, Singapore 0820
Tel: (65) 2987033 Telex: RS 39904
Fax: (65) 2969209

Printed in Great Britain by Athenacum Press Ltd, Gateshead, Tyne & Wear

The publishers would like to thank the following for permission to reproduce photographs:
The Bodleian Library: p.171, 172; Dulwich Picture Gallery: p.170 (top);
Fitzwilliam Museum: p.170 (bottom); Victoria and Albert Museum Picture Library: p.173

The cover illustration is by Susan Scott.

Contents

Acknowledgements

I would like to thank Robert Scriven and Mary Worrall of Oxr
University Press and Dr Victor Lee of the Open University for the
advice about the preparation of this book. I am also grateful to
Gillian Walters who did the typing.
The people who have most helped me to think about Donne are my
past pupils. They have listened, contributed and argued with me for
well over ten years, and I am greatly indebted to them for keeping
alive the questions about this puzzling yet rewarding body of work.
As they are too numerous to mention by name, I shall select three
whose remarks I remember to have been particularly helpful and
stimulating - Fiona Chamberlain, Margaret Finch, and David Roe.

Richard Gill

Editors

Dr Victor Lee

Victor Lee, the series editor, read English at University College,
Cardiff. He was later awarded his doctorate at the University of
Oxford. He has taught at secondary and tertiary level, and is
currently working at the Open University. There, he has been
involved in the making of a considerable number of texts, television
and radio programmes. Victor Lee's experience as an examiner is
very wide: he has been a Chief Examiner in English at 'A' level for
three different boards stretching over a period of twenty years.

Richard Gill

Richard Gill is Head of English at Wyggeston and Queen Elizabeth
I College, Leicester.

Foreword

Oxford Student Texts are specifically aimed at presenting poetry and drama to an audience which is studying English Literature at an advanced level. Each text is designed as an integrated whole consisting of three main parts. The poetry or the play is always placed first to stress its importance and to encourage students to enjoy it without secondary critical material of any kind. When help is needed on other occasions, the second and third parts of these texts, the Notes and the Approaches provide it.

The Notes perform two functions. First, they provide information and explain allusions. Secondly, and this is where they differ from most texts at this level, they often raise questions of central concern to the interpretation of the poem or the play being dealt with, particularly in the use of a general note placed at the beginning of the particular notes.

The third part, the Approaches section, deals with major issues of response to the particular selection of poetry or drama, as opposed to the work of the writer as a whole. One of the major aims of this part of the text is to emphasize that there is no one right answer to interpretation, but a series of approaches. Readers are given guidance as to what counts as evidence, but, in the end, left to make up their mind as to which are the most suitable interpretations, or to add their own.

To help achieve this, the Approaches section contains a number of activity-discussion sequences, although it must be stressed that these are optional. Significant issues about the poetry or the play are raised in these activities. Readers are invited to tackle these activities before proceeding to the discussion section where possible responses to the questions raised in the activities are considered. Their main function is to engage readers actively in the ideas of the text. However, these activity-discussion sequences are so arranged that, if readers wish to treat the Approaches as continuous prose and not attempt the activities, they can.

At the end of each text there is also a list of tasks. Whereas the activity-discussion sequences are aimed at increasing understanding of the literary work itself, these tasks are intended to help explore ideas about the poetry or the play after the student has completed the reading of the work and the studying of the Notes and Approaches. These tasks are particularly helpful for coursework projects or in preparing for an examination.

Victor Lee *Series Editor*

Songs and Sonnets

The Anniversary

All kings, and all their favourites,
　　All glory of honours, beauties, wits,
The sun itself, which makes times, as they pass,
Is elder by a year, now, than it was
When thou and I first one another saw:
All other things, to their destruction draw,
　　Only our love hath no decay;
This, no tomorrow hath, nor yesterday,
Running it never runs from us away,
10　But truly keeps his first, last, everlasting day.

Two graves must hide thine and my corse,
　　If one might, death were no divorce,
Alas, as well as other princes, we,
(Who prince enough in one another be,)
Must leave at last in death, these eyes, and ears,
Oft fed with true oaths, and with sweet salt tears;
　　But souls where nothing dwells but love
(All other thoughts being inmates) then shall prove
This, or a love increased there above,
20　When bodies to their graves, souls from their graves
　　　　remove.

And then we shall be throughly blessed,
　　But we no more, than all the rest.
Here upon earth, we are kings, and none but we
Can be such kings, nor of such subjects be;
Who is so safe as we? where none can do
Treason to us, except one of us two.
　　True and false fears let us refrain,
Let us love nobly, and live, and add again
Years and years unto years, till we attain
30　To write threescore, this is the second of our reign.

The Apparition

When by thy scorn, O murderess, I am dead,
And that thou think'st thee free
From all solicitation from me,
Then shall my ghost come to thy bed,
And thee, feigned vestal, in worse arms shall see;
Then thy sick taper will begin to wink,
And he, whose thou art then, being tired before,
Will, if thou stir, or pinch to wake him, think
    Thou call'st for more,
10 And in false sleep will from thee shrink,
And then poor aspen wretch, neglected thou
Bathed in a cold quicksilver sweat wilt lie
    A verier ghost than I;
What I will say, I will not tell thee now,
Lest that preserve thee; and since my love is spent,
I had rather thou shouldst painfully repent,
Than by my threatenings rest still innocent.

The Canonization

For God's sake hold your tongue, and let me love,
    Or chide my palsy, or my gout,
My five grey hairs, or ruined fortune flout,
      With wealth your state, your mind with arts
      improve,
      Take you a course, get you a place,
      Observe his Honour, or his Grace,
Or the King's real, or his stamped face
    Contemplate; what you will, approve,
    So you will let me love.

10 Alas, alas, who's injured by my love?
      What merchant's ships have my sighs drowned?
Who says my tears have overflowed his ground?
      When did my colds a forward spring remove?
        When did the heats which my veins fill
        Add one more to the plaguy bill?
Soldiers find wars, and lawyers find out still
    Litigious men, which quarrels move,
    Though she and I do love.

Call us what you will, we are made such by love;
20   Call her one, me another fly,
We are tapers too, and at our own cost die,
      And we in us find the eagle and the dove,
        The phoenix riddle hath more wit
        By us; we two being one, are it.
So to one neutral thing both sexes fit
    We die and rise the same, and prove
    Mysterious by this love.

We can die by it, if not live by love,
   And if unfit for tombs and hearse
30 Our legend be, it will be fit for verse;
   And if no piece of chronicle we prove,
      We'll build in sonnets pretty rooms;
      As well a well wrought urn becomes
   The greatest ashes, as half-acre tombs,
      And by these hymns, all shall approve
      Us canonized for love:

   And thus invoke us; 'You whom reverend love
      Made one another's hermitage;
   You, to whom love was peace, that now is rage;
40   Who did the whole world's soul contract, and
         drove
         Into the glasses of your eyes
         (So made such mirrors, and such spies,
   That they did all to you epitomize,)
         Countries, towns, courts: beg from above
         A pattern of your love!'

The Damp

When I am dead, and doctors know not why,
    And my friends' curiosity
Will have me cut up to survey each part,
When they shall find your picture in my heart,
    You think a sudden damp of love
    Will through all their senses move,
And work on them as me, and so prefer
Your murder, to the name of massacre.

Poor victories; but if you dare be brave,
10   And pleasure in your conquest have,
First kill th' enormous giant, your Disdain,
And let th' enchantress Honour, next be slain,
    And like a Goth and Vandal rise,
    Deface records, and histories
Of your own arts and triumphs over men,
And without such advantage kill me then.

For I could muster up as well as you
    My giants, and my witches too,
Which are vast Constancy, and Secretness,
20 But these I neither look for, nor profess;
    Kill me as woman, let me die
    As a mere man; do you but try
Your passive valour, and you shall find then,
Naked you have odds enough of any man.

The Dream

Dear love, for nothing less than thee
Would I have broke this happy dream,
    It was a theme
For reason, much too strong for phantasy,
Therefore thou waked'st me wisely; yet
My dream thou brok'st not, but continued'st it:
Thou art so true, that thoughts of thee suffice,
To make dreams truths, and fables histories;
Enter these arms, for since thou thought'st it best,
10 Not to dream all my dream, let's act the rest.

As lightning, or a taper's light,
Thine eyes, and not thy noise waked me;
    Yet I thought thee
(For thou lov'st truth) an angel, at first sight,
But when I saw thou saw'st my heart,
And knew'st my thoughts, beyond an angel's art,
When thou knew'st what I dreamed, when thou
    knew'st when
Excess of joy would wake me, and cam'st then,
I must confess, it could not choose but be
20 Profane, to think thee anything but thee.

Coming and staying showed thee, thee,
But rising makes me doubt, that now,
    Thou art not thou.
That love is weak, where fear's as strong as he;
'Tis not all spirit, pure, and brave,
If mixture it of fear, shame, honour, have.
Perchance as torches which must ready be,
Men light and put out, so thou deal'st with me,
Thou cam'st to kindle, goest to come; then I
30 Will dream that hope again, but else would die.

The Ecstasy

Where, like a pillow on a bed,
    A pregnant bank swelled up, to rest
The violet's reclining head,
    Sat we two, one another's best;

Our hands were firmly cemented
    With a fast balm, which thence did spring,
Our eye-beams twisted, and did thread
    Our eyes, upon one double string;

So to' intergraft our hands, as yet
10   Was all our means to make us one,
And pictures in our eyes to get
    Was all our propagation.

As 'twixt two equal armies, Fate
    Suspends uncertain victory,
Our souls, (which to advance their state,
    Were gone out), hung 'twixt her, and me.

And whilst our souls negotiate there,
    We like sepulchral statues lay;
All day, the same our postures were,
20   And we said nothing, all the day.

If any, so by love refined,
    That he soul's language understood,
And by good love were grown all mind,
    Within convenient distance stood,

He (though he knew not which soul spake
    Because both meant, both spake the same)
Might thence a new concoction take,
    And part far purer than he came.

This ecstasy doth unperplex
30   (We said) and tell us what we love,
We see by this, it was not sex,
    We see, we saw not what did move:

But as all several souls contain
    Mixture of things, they know not what,
Love, these mixed souls doth mix again,
    And makes both one, each this and that.

A single violet transplant,
    The strength, the colour, and the size,
(All which before was poor, and scant,)
40   Redoubles still, and multiplies.

When love, with one another so
    Interinanimates two souls,
That abler soul, which thence doth flow,
    Defects of loneliness controls.

We then, who are this new soul, know,
    Of what we are composed, and made,
For, th' atomies of which we grow,
    Are souls, whom no change can invade.

But O alas, so long, so far
50   Our bodies why do we forbear?
They are ours, though they are not we, we are
    The intelligences, they the sphere.

We owe them thanks, because they thus,
    Did us, to us, at first convey,
Yielded their forces, sense, to us,
    Nor are dross to us, but allay.

On man heaven's influence works not so,
    But that it first imprints the air,
So soul into the soul may flow,
60   Though it to body first repair.

As our blood labours to beget
    Spirits, as like souls as it can,
Because such fingers need to knit
    That subtle knot, which makes us man:

So must pure lovers' souls descend
    T' affections, and to faculties,
Which sense may reach and apprehend,
    Else a great prince in prison lies.

To our bodies turn we then, that so
70   Weak men on love revealed may look;
Love's mysteries in souls do grow,
    But yet the body is his book.

And if some lover, such as we,
    Have heard this dialogue of one,
Let him still mark us, he shall see
    Small change, when we'are to bodies gone.

The Expiration

So, so, break off this last lamenting kiss,
    Which sucks two souls, and vapours both away,
Turn thou ghost that way, and let me turn this,
    And let ourselves benight our happiest day,
We asked none leave to love; nor will we owe
    Any, so cheap a death, as saying, Go;

Go; and if that word have not quite killed thee,
    Ease me with death, by bidding me go too.
Oh, if it have, let my word work on me,
10   And a just office on a murderer do.
Except it be too late, to kill me so,
    Being double dead, going, and bidding, go.

A Fever

Oh do not die, for I shall hate
    All women so, when thou art gone,
That thee I shall not celebrate,
    When I remember, thou wast one.

But yet thou canst not die, I know,
    To leave this world behind, is death,
But when thou from this world wilt go,
    The whole world vapours with thy breath.

Or if, when thou, the world's soul, go'st,
10   It stay, 'tis but thy carcase then,
The fairest woman, but thy ghost,
    But corrupt worms, the worthiest men.

Oh wrangling schools, that search what fire
    Shall burn this world, had none the wit
Unto this knowledge to aspire,
    That this her fever might be it?

And yet she cannot waste by this,
    Nor long bear this torturing wrong,
For much corruption needful is
20   To fuel such a fever long.

These burning fits but meteors be,
    Whose matter in thee is soon spent.
Thy beauty, and all parts, which are thee,
    Are unchangeable firmament.

Yet 'twas of my mind, seizing thee,
    Though it in thee cannot perséver.
For I had rather owner be
    Of thee one hour, than all else ever.

The Flea

Mark but this flea, and mark in this,
How little that which thou deny'st me is;
Me it sucked first, and now sucks thee,
And in this flea, our two bloods mingled be;
Confess it, this cannot be said
A sin, or shame, or loss of maidenhead,
    Yet this enjoys before it woo,
    And pampered swells with one blood made of two,
And this, alas, is more than we would do.

10 Oh stay, three lives in one flea spare,
Where we almost, nay more than married are.
This flea is you and I, and this
Our marriage bed, and marriage temple is;
Though parents grudge, and you, we'are met,
And cloistered in these living walls of jet.
    Though use make you apt to kill me,
    Let not to this, self murder added be,
    And sacrilege, three sins in killing three.

Cruel and sudden, hast thou since
20 Purpled thy nail, in blood of innocence?
In what could this flea guilty be,
Except in that drop which it sucked from thee?
Yet thou triumph'st, and say'st that thou
Find'st not thyself, nor me the weaker now;
    'Tis true, then learn how false, fears be;
    Just so much honour, when thou yield'st to me,
    Will waste, as this flea's death took life from thee.

The Funeral

Whoever comes to shroud me, do not harm
      Nor question much
That subtle wreath of hair, which crowns my arm;
The mystery, the sign you must not touch,
      For 'tis my outward soul,
Viceroy to that, which then to heaven being gone,
      Will leave this to control,
And keep these limbs, her provinces, from dissolution.

For if the sinewy thread my brain lets fall
10   Through every part,
Can tie those parts, and make me one of all;
These hairs which upward grew, and strength and art
      Have from a better brain,
Can better do it; except she meant that I
      By this should know my pain,
As prisoners then are manacled, when they are
      condemned to die.

Whate'er she meant by it, bury it with me,
      For since I am
Love's martyr, it might breed idolatry,
20 If into others' hands these relics came;
      As 'twas humility
To afford to it all that a soul can do,
      So, 'tis some bravery,
That since you would save none of me, I bury some
      of you.

The Good Morrow

I wonder by my troth, what thou, and I
   Did, till we loved? were we not weaned till then,
But sucked on country pleasures, childishly?
   Or snorted we in the seven sleepers' den?
'Twas so; but this, all pleasures fancies be.
If ever any beauty I did see,
Which I desired, and got, 'twas but a dream of thee.

And now good morrow to our waking souls,
   Which watch not one another out of fear;
10   For love, all love of other sights controls,
   And makes one little room, an every where.
Let sea-discoverers to new worlds have gone,
Let maps to others, worlds on worlds have shown,
Let us possess one world, each hath one, and is one.

My face in thine eye, thine in mine appears,
   And true plain hearts do in the faces rest,
Where can we find two better hemispheres
   Without sharp north, without declining west?
What ever dies, was not mixed equally;
20   If our two loves be one, or, thou and I
Love so alike, that none do slacken, none can die.

A Jet Ring Sent

Thou art not so black, as my heart,
Nor half so brittle, as her heart, thou art;
What wouldst thou say? Shall both our properties by
    thee be spoke,
Nothing more endless, nothing sooner broke?

Marriage rings are not of this stuff;
Oh, why should aught less precious, or less tough
Figure our loves? Except in thy name thou have bid it say,
    I am cheap, and naught but fashion, fling me away.

Yet stay with me since thou art come,
10   Circle this finger's top, which didst her thumb.
Be justly proud, and gladly safe, that thou dost dwell
    with me,
She that, oh, broke her faith, would soon break thee.

Lovers' Infiniteness

If yet I have not all thy love,
Dear, I shall never have it all,
I cannot breathe one other sigh, to move,
Nor can entreat one other tear to fall.
All my treasure, which should purchase thee,
Sighs, tears, and oaths, and letters I have spent,
Yet no more can be due to me,
Than at the bargain made was meant.
If then thy gift of love were partial,
10 That some to me, some should to others fall,
    Dear, I shall never have thee all.

Or if then thou gavest me all,
All was but all, which thou hadst then;
But if in thy heart, since, there be or shall
New love created be, by other men,
Which have their stocks entire, and can in tears,
In sighs, in oaths, and letters outbid me,
This new love may beget new fears,
For, this love was not vowed by thee.
20 And yet it was, thy gift being general,
The ground, thy heart is mine; whatever shall
    Grow there, dear, I should have it all.

Yet I would not have all yet,
He that hath all can have no more,
And since my love doth every day admit
New growth, thou shouldst have new rewards in
    store;
Thou canst not every day give me thy heart,
If thou canst give it, then thou never gav'st it:
Love's riddles are, that though thy heart depart,
30 It stays at home, and thou with losing sav'st it:
But we will have a way more liberal,
Than changing hearts, to join them, so we shall
    Be one, and one another's all.

Love's Alchemy

Some that have deeper digged love's mine than I,
Say, where his centric happiness doth lie:
    I have loved, and got, and told,
But should I love, get, tell, till I were old,
I should not find that hidden mystery;
    Oh, 'tis imposture all:
And as no chemic yet the elixir got,
    But glorifies his pregnant pot,
    If by the way to him befall
10 Some odoriferous thing, or medicinal,
    So, lovers dream a rich and long delight,
    But get a winter-seeming summer's night.

Our ease, our thrift, our honour, and our day,
Shall we, for this vain bubble's shadow pay?
    Ends love in this, that my man,
Can be as happy as I can; if he can
Endure the short scorn of a bridegroom's play?
    That loving wretch that swears,
'Tis not the bodies marry, but the minds,
20 Which he in her angelic finds,
Would swear as justly, that he hears,
In that day's rude hoarse minstrelsy, the spheres.
Hope not for mind in women; at their best
    Sweetness and wit, they are but mummy, possessed.

Love's Growth

I scarce believe my love to be so pure
    As I had thought it was,
    Because it doth endure
Vicissitude, and season, as the grass;
Methinks I lied all winter, when I swore,
My love was infinite, if spring make it more.
But if this medicine, love, which cures all sorrow
With more, not only be no quintessence,
But mixed of all stuffs, paining soul, or sense,
10   And of the sun his working vigour borrow,
Love's not so pure, and abstract, as they use
To say, which have no mistress but their Muse,
But as all else, being elemented too,
Love sometimes would contemplate, sometimes do.

And yet not greater, but more eminent,
    Love by the spring is grown;
    As, in the firmament,
Stars by the sun are not enlarged, but shown,
Gentle love deeds, as blossoms on a bough,
20   From love's awakened root do bud out now.
If, as in water stirred more circles be
Produced by one, love such additions take,
Those like so many spheres, but one heaven make,
For, they are all concentric unto thee,
And though each spring do add to love new heat,
As princes do in times of action get
New taxes, and remit them not in peace,
No winter shall abate the spring's increase.

A Nocturnal upon S. Lucy's Day, being the shortest day

'Tis the year's midnight, and it is the day's,
Lucy's, who scarce seven hours herself unmasks,
    The sun is spent, and now his flasks
     Send forth light squibs, no constant rays;
       The world's whole sap is sunk:
The general balm th' hydroptic earth hath drunk,
Whither, as to the bed's-feet, life is shrunk,
Dead and interred; yet all these seem to laugh,
Compared with me, who am their epitaph.

10 Study me then, you who shall lovers be
At the next world, that is, at the next spring:
    For I am every dead thing,
     In whom love wrought new alchemy.
      For his art did express
A quintessence even from nothingness,
From dull privations, and lean emptiness
He ruined me, and I am re-begot
Of absence, darkness, death; things which are not.

All others, from all things, draw all that's good,
20 Life, soul, form, spirit, whence they being have;
    I, by love's limbeck, am the grave
     Of all, that's nothing. Oft a flood
      Have we two wept, and so
Drowned the whole world, us two; oft did we grow
To be two chaoses, when we did show
Care to aught else; and often absences
Withdrew our souls, and made us carcases.

But I am by her death (which word wrongs her)
Of the first nothing, the elixir grown;
30   Were I a man, that I were one,
        I needs must know; I should prefer,
            If I were any beast,
Some ends, some means; yea plants, yea stones
        detest,
And love; all, all some properties invest;
If I an ordinary nothing were,
As shadow, a light, and body must be here.

But I am none; nor will my sun renew.
You lovers, for whose sake, the lesser sun
        At this time to the Goat is run
40   To fetch new lust, and give it you,
            Enjoy your summer all;
Since she enjoys her long night's festival,
Let me prepare towards her, and let me call
This hour her vigil, and her eve, since this
Both the year's, and the day's deep midnight is.

The Relic

When my grave is broke up again
Some second guest to entertain,
(For graves have learned that woman-head
To be to more than one a bed)
    And he that digs it, spies
A bracelet of bright hair about the bone,
      Will he not let us alone,
And think that there a loving couple lies,
Who thought that this device might be some way
10 To make their souls, at the last busy day,
Meet at this grave, and make a little stay?

      If this fall in a time, or land,
      Where mis-devotion doth command,
      Then, he that digs us up, will bring
      Us, to the Bishop, and the King,
        To make us relics; then
Thou shalt be a Mary Magdalen, and I
      A something else thereby;
All women shall adore us, and some men;
20 And since at such time, miracles are sought,
I would have that age by this paper taught
What miracles we harmless lovers wrought.

      First, we loved well and faithfully,
      Yet knew not what we loved, nor why,
      Difference of sex no more we knew,
      Than our guardian angels do;
        Coming and going, we
Perchance might kiss, but not between those meals;
      Our hands ne'er touched the seals,
30 Which nature, injured by late law, sets free:
These miracles we did; but now alas,
All measure, and all language, I should pass,
Should I tell what a miracle she was.

Song

Go, and catch a falling star,
    Get with child a mandrake root,
Tell me, where all past years are,
    Or who cleft the Devil's foot,
Teach me to hear mermaids singing,
    Or to keep off envy's stinging,
        And find
        What wind
Serves to advance an honest mind.

10 If thou be'est born to strange sights,
        Things invisible to see,
    Ride ten thousand days and nights,
        Till age snow white hairs on thee,
    Thou, when thou return'st, wilt tell me
    All strange wonders that befell thee,
            And swear
            No where
    Lives a woman true, and fair.

    If thou find'st one, let me know,
20   Such a pilgrimage were sweet,
    Yet do not, I would not go,
        Though at next door we might meet,
    Though she were true, when you met her,
    And last, till you write your letter,
            Yet she
            Will be
    False, ere I come, to two, or three.

Song

Sweetest love, I do not go,
    For weariness of thee,
Nor in hope the world can show
    A fitter love for me;
      But since that I
Must die at last, 'tis best,
To use my self in jest
    Thus by feigned deaths to die.

Yesternight the sun went hence,
10   And yet is here today,
He hath no desire nor sense,
    Nor half so short a way:
      Then fear not me,
But believe that I shall make
Speedier journeys, since I take
    More wings and spurs than he.

O how feeble is man's power,
    That if good fortune fall,
Cannot add another hour,
20   Nor a lost hour recall!
      But come bad chance,
And we join to it our strength,
And we teach it art and length,
    Itself o'er us to advance.

When thou sigh'st, thou sigh'st not wind,
    But sigh'st my soul away,
When thou weep'st, unkindly kind,
    My life's blood doth decay.

It cannot be
30   That thou lov'st me, as thou say'st,
If in thine my life thou waste,
    Thou art the best of me.

Let not thy divining heart
    Forethink me any ill,
Destiny may take thy part,
    And may thy fears fulfil;
    But think that we
Are but turned aside to sleep;
They who one another keep
40   Alive, ne'er parted be.

The Sun Rising

    Busy old fool, unruly sun,
      Why dost thou thus,
Through windows, and through curtains call on us?
Must to thy motions lovers' seasons run?
    Saucy pedantic wretch, go chide
    Late school-boys, and sour prentices,
    Go tell court-huntsmen, that the King will ride,
    Call country ants to harvest offices;
Love, all alike, no season knows, nor clime,
10   Nor hours, days, months, which are the rags of time.

    Thy beams, so reverend, and strong
      Why shouldst thou think?
I could eclipse and cloud them with a wink,
But that I would not lose her sight so long:
    If her eyes have not blinded thine,

   Look, and tomorrow late, tell me,
   Whether both th'Indias of spice and mine
   Be where thou left'st them, or lie here with me.
  Ask for those kings whom thou saw'st yesterday,
20 And thou shalt hear, All here in one bed lay.

   She'is all states, and all princes, I,
   Nothing else is.
  Princes do but play us; compared to this,
  All honour's mimic; all wealth alchemy.
   Thou sun art half as happy as we,
   In that the world's contracted thus;
   Thine age asks ease, and since thy duties be
   To warm the world, that's done in warming us.
  Shine here to us, and thou art everywhere;
30 This bed thy centre is, these walls, thy sphere.

The Triple Fool

   I am two fools, I know,
  For loving, and for saying so
   In whining poetry;
  But where's that wiseman, that would not be I,
   If she would not deny?
  Then as th'earth's inward narrow crooked lanes
  Do purge sea water's fretful salt away,
   I thought, if I could draw my pains
  Through rhyme's vexation, I should them allay.
10 Grief brought to numbers cannot be so fierce,
  For, he tames it, that fetters it in verse

But when I have done so,
Some man, his art and voice to show,
   Doth set and sing my pain,
And, by delighting many, frees again
   Grief, which verse did restrain.
To love and grief tribute of verse belongs,
But not of such as pleases when 'tis read,
   Both are increased by such songs:
20 For both their triumphs so are published,
And I, which was two fools, do so grow three;
Who are a little wise, the best fools be.

Twicknam Garden

Blasted with sighs, and surrounded with tears,
   Hither I come to seek the spring,
   And at mine eyes, and at mine ears,
Receive such balms, as else cure everything;
   But O, self traitor, I do bring
The spider love, which transubstantiates all,
   And can convert manna to gall,
And that this place may thoroughly be thought
   True paradise, I have the serpent brought.

10 'Twere wholesomer for me, that winter did
   Benight the glory of this place,
   And that a grave frost did forbid
These trees to laugh, and mock me to my face;
   But that I may not this disgrace
Endure, nor yet leave loving, Love, let me
   Some senseless piece of this place be;
Make me a mandrake, so I may groan here,
   Or a stone fountain weeping out my year.

Hither with crystal vials, lovers come,
20   And take my tears, which are love's wine,
And try your mistress' tears at home,
For all are false, that taste not just like mine;
      Alas, hearts do not in eyes shine,
Nor can you more judge woman's thoughts by tears,
      Than by her shadow, what she wears.
O perverse sex, where none is true but she,
      Who's therefore true, because her truth kills me.

The Undertaking

I have done one braver thing
      Than all the Worthies did,
And yet a braver thence doth spring,
      Which is, to keep that hid.

It were but madness now t'impart
      The skill of specular stone,
When he which can have learned the art
      To cut it, can find none.

So, if I now should utter this,
10   Others (because no more
Such stuff to work upon, there is,)
      Would love but as before.

But he who loveliness within
      Hath found, all outward loathes,
For he who colour loves, and skin,
      Loves but their oldest clothes.

If, as I have, you also do
    Virtue attired in woman see,
And dare love that, and say so too,
20   And forget the He and She;

And if this love, though placed so,
    From profane men you hide,
Which will no faith on this bestow,
    Or, if they do, deride:

Then you have done a braver thing
    Than all the Worthies did,
And a braver thence will spring,
    Which is, to keep that hid.

A Valediction: forbidding Mourning

As virtuous men pass mildly away,
    And whisper to their souls, to go,
Whilst some of their sad friends do say,
    The breath goes now, and some say, no:

So let us melt, and make no noise,
    No tear-floods, nor sigh-tempests move,
'Twere profanation of our joys
    To tell the laity our love.

Moving of th' earth brings harms and fears,
10   Men reckon what it did and meant,
But trepidation of the spheres,
    Though greater far, is innocent.

Dull sublunary lovers' love
    (Whose soul is sense) cannot admit
Absence, because it doth remove
    Those things which elemented it.

But we by a love, so much refined,
    That our selves know not what it is,
Inter-assured of the mind,
20   Care less, eyes, lips, and hands to miss.

Our two souls therefore, which are one,
    Though I must go, endure not yet
A breach, but an expansion,
    Like gold to aery thinness beat.

If they be two, they are two so
    As stiff twin compasses are two,
Thy soul the fixed foot, makes no show
    To move, but doth, if th'other do.

And though it in the centre sit,
30   Yet when the other far doth roam,
It leans, and hearkens after it,
    And grows erect, as that comes home.

Such wilt thou be to me, who must
    Like th' other foot, obliquely run;
Thy firmness makes my circle just,
    And makes me end, where I begun.

Woman's Constancy

Now thou hast loved me one whole day,
Tomorrow when thou leav'st, what wilt thou say?
Wilt thou then antedate some new made vow?
     Or say that now
We are not just those persons, which we were?
Or, that oaths made in reverential fear
Of Love, and his wrath, any may forswear?
Or, as true deaths, true marriages untie,
So lovers' contracts, images of those,
10 Bind but till sleep, death's image, them unloose?
     Or, your own end to justify,
For having purposed change, and falsehood, you
Can have no way but falsehood to be true?
Vain lunatic, against these 'scapes I could
     Dispute, and conquer, if I would,
     Which I abstain to do,
For by tomorrow, I may think so too.

Elegies

Elegy 4: The Perfume

Once, and but once found in thy company,
All thy supposed escapes are laid on me;
And as a thief at bar, is questioned there
By all the men, that have been robbed that year,
So am I, (by this traitorous means surprised)
By thy hydroptic father catechized.
Though he had wont to search with glazed eyes,
As though he came to kill a cockatrice,
Though he have oft sworn, that he would remove
10 Thy beauty's beauty, and food of our love,
Hope of his goods, if I with thee were seen,
Yet close and secret, as our souls, we have been.
Though thy immortal mother which doth lie
Still buried in her bed, yet will not die,
Takes this advantage to sleep out day-light,
And watch thy entries, and returns all night,
And, when she takes thy hand, and would seem kind,
Doth search what rings, and armlets she can find,
And kissing notes the colour of thy face,
20 And fearing less thou art swoll'n, doth thee embrace;
To try if thou long, doth name strange meats,
And notes thy paleness, blushing, sighs, and sweats;
And politicly will to thee confess
The sins of her own youth's rank lustiness;
Yet love these sorceries did remove, and move
Thee to gull thine own mother for my love.
Thy little brethren, which like faery sprites
Oft skipped into our chamber, those sweet nights,
And kissed, and ingled on thy father's knee,
30 Were bribed next day, to tell what they did see.
The grim eight-foot-high iron-bound serving-man,

That oft names God in oaths, and only then,
He that to bar the first gate, doth as wide
As the great Rhodian Colossus stride,
Which, if in hell no other pains there were,
Makes me fear hell, because he must be there:
Though by thy father he were hired to this,
Could never witness any touch or kiss.
But Oh, too common ill, I brought with me
40   That, which betrayed me to mine enemy:
A loud perfume, which at my entrance cried
Even at thy father's nose, so we were spied.
When, like a tyrant king, that in his bed
Smelt gunpowder, the pale wretch shivered.
Had it been some bad smell, he would have thought
That his own feet, or breath, that smell had wrought.
But as we in our isle imprisoned,
Where cattle only, and diverse dogs are bred,
The precious unicorns, strange monsters call,
50   So thought he good, strange, that had none at all.
I taught my silks, their whistling to forbear,
Even my oppressed shoes, dumb and speechless were,
Only, thou bitter sweet, whom I had laid
Next me, me traitorously hast betrayed,
And unsuspected hast invisibly
At once fled unto him, and stayed with me.
Base excrement of earth, which dost confound
Sense, from distinguishing the sick from sound;
By thee the silly amorous sucks his death
60   By drawing in a leprous harlot's breath;
By thee, the greatest stain to man's estate
Falls on us, to be called effeminate;
Though you be much loved in the prince's hall,
There, things that seem, exceed substantial.
Gods, when ye fumed on altars, were pleased well,

Because you were burnt, not that they liked your
    smell;
You are loathsome all, being taken simply alone,
Shall we love ill things joined, and hate each one?
If you were good, your good doth soon decay;
70 And you are rare, that takes the good away.
All my perfumes, I give most willingly
To embalm thy father's corse; What? will he die?

Elegy 5: His Picture

Here take my picture, though I bid farewell;
Thine, in my heart, where my soul dwells, shall
    dwell.
'Tis like me now, but I dead, 'twill be more
When we are shadows both, than 'twas before.
When weather-beaten I come back; my hand,
Perhaps with rude oars torn, or sun-beams tanned,
My face and breast of haircloth, and my head
With care's rash sudden hoariness o'erspread,
My body a sack of bones, broken within,
10 And powder's blue stains scattered on my skin;
If rival fools tax thee to have loved a man,
So foul, and coarse, as oh, I may seem then,
This shall say what I was: and thou shalt say,
Do his hurts reach me? doth my worth decay?
Or do they reach his judging mind, that he
Should now love less, what he did love to see?
That which in him was fair and delicate,
Was but the milk, which in love's childish state
Did nurse it: who now is grown strong enough
20 To feed on that, which to disused tastes seems tough.

Elegy 16: On his Mistress

By our first strange and fatal interview,
By all desires which thereof did ensue,
By our long starving hopes, by that remorse
Which my words' masculine persuasive force
Begot in thee, and by the memory
Of hurts, which spies and rivals threatened me,
I calmly beg: but by thy father's wrath,
By all pains, which want and divorcement hath,
I conjure thee; and all the oaths which I
10 And thou have sworn to seal joint constancy,
Here I unswear, and overswear them thus,
Thou shalt not love by ways so dangerous.
Temper, O fair love, love's impetuous rage,
Be my true mistress still, not my feigned page;
I'll go, and, by thy kind leave, leave behind
Thee, only worthy to nurse in my mind
Thirst to come back; oh, if thou die before,
From other lands my soul towards thee shall soar,
Thy (else almighty) beauty cannot move
20 Rage from the seas, nor thy love teach them love,
Nor tame wild Boreas' harshness; thou hast read
How roughly he in pieces shivered
Fair Orithea, whom he swore he loved.
Fall ill or good, 'tis madness to have proved
Dangers unurged; feed on this flattery,
That absent lovers one in th' other be.
Dissemble nothing, not a boy, nor change
Thy body's habit, nor mind's; be not strange
To thy self only; all will spy in thy face
30 A blushing womanly discovering grace;
Richly clothed apes, are called apes, and as soon

Eclipsed as bright we call the moon the moon.
Men of France, changeable chameleons,
Spitals of diseases, shops of fashions,
Love's fuellers, and the rightest company
Of players, which upon the world's stage be,
Will quickly know thee, and know thee; and alas
Th' indifferent Italian, as we pass
His warm land, well content to think thee page,
40 Will hunt thee with such lust, and hideous rage,
As Lot's fair guests were vexed. But none of these
Nor spongy hydroptic Dutch shall thee displease,
If thou stay here. Oh stay here, for, for thee
England is only a worthy gallery,
To walk in expectation, till from thence
Our greatest King call thee to his presence.
When I am gone, dream me some happiness,
Nor let thy looks our long-hid love confess,
Nor praise, nor dispraise me, nor bless nor curse
50 Openly love's force, nor in bed fright thy nurse
With midnight's startings, crying out, 'Oh, oh
Nurse, O my love is slain, I saw him go
O'er the white Alps alone; I saw him, I,
Assailed, fight, taken, stabbed, bleed, fall, and die.'
Augur me better chance, except dread Jove
Think it enough for me to have had thy love.

Elegy 19: To his Mistress Going to Bed

Come, Madam, come, all rest my powers defy,
Until I labour, I in labour lie.
The foe oft-times having the foe in sight,

Is tired with standing though he never fight.
Off with that girdle, like heaven's zone glistering,
But a far fairer world encompassing.
Unpin that spangled breastplate which you wear,
That th' eyes of busy fools may be stopped there.
Unlace yourself, for that harmonious chime
10 Tells me from you, that now 'tis your bed time.
Off with that happy busk, which I envy,
That still can be, and still can stand so nigh.
Your gown going off, such beauteous state reveals,
As when from flowery meads th' hill's shadow steals.
Off with that wiry coronet and show
The hairy diadem which on you doth grow;
Now off with those shoes, and then safely tread
In this love's hallowed temple, this soft bed.
In such white robes heaven's angels used to be
20 Received by men; thou angel bring'st with thee
A heaven like Mahomet's paradise; and though
Ill spirits walk in white, we easily know
By this these angels from an evil sprite,
Those set our hairs, but these our flesh upright.
　　　License my roving hands, and let them go
Before, behind, between, above, below.
O my America, my new found land,
My kingdom, safeliest when with one man manned,
My mine of precious stones, my empery,
30 How blessed am I in this discovering thee!
To enter in these bonds, is to be free;
Then where my hand is set, my seal shall be.
　　　Full nakedness, all joys are due to thee.
As souls unbodied, bodies unclothed must be,
To taste whole joys. Gems which you women use
Are like Atlanta's balls, cast in men's views,
That when a fool's eye lighteth on a gem,

His earthly soul may covet theirs, not them.
Like pictures, or like books' gay coverings made
40 For laymen, are all women thus arrayed;
Themselves are mystic books, which only we
Whom their imputed grace will dignify
Must see revealed. Then since I may know,
As liberally, as to a midwife, show
Thyself: cast all, yea, this white linen hence,
Here is no penance, much less innocence.

     To teach thee, I am naked first, why then
What needst thou have more covering than a man.

Religious Poems

Holy sonnets

6

This is my play's last scene, here heavens appoint
My pilgrimage's last mile; and my race
Idly, yet quickly run, hath this last pace,
My span's last inch, my minute's latest point,
And gluttonous death, will instantly unjoint
My body, and soul, and I shall sleep a space,
But my'ever-waking part shall see that face,
Whose fear already shakes my every joint:
Then, as my soul, to heaven her first seat, takes flight,
10 And earth-born body, in the earth shall dwell,
So, fall my sins, that all may have their right,
To where they are bred, and would press me, to hell.
Impute me righteous, thus purged of evil,
For thus I leave the world, the flesh, and devil.

7

At the round earth's imagined corners, blow
Your trumpets, angels, and arise, arise
From death, you numberless infinities
Of souls, and to your scattered bodies go,
All whom the flood did, and fire shall o'erthrow,
All whom war, dearth, age, agues, tyrannies,
Despair, law, chance, hath slain, and you whose eyes,
Shall behold God, and never taste death's woe.
But let them sleep, Lord, and me mourn a space,
10 For, if above all these, my sins abound,
'Tis late to ask abundance of thy grace,
When we are there; here on this lowly ground,
Teach me how to repent; for that's as good
As if thou hadst sealed my pardon, with thy blood.

10

Death be not proud, though some have called thee
Mighty and dreadful, for, thou art not so,
For, those, whom thou think'st, thou dost
    overthrow,
Die not, poor death, nor yet canst thou kill me;
From rest and sleep, which but thy pictures be,
Much pleasure, then from thee, much more must
    flow,
And soonest our best men with thee do go,
Rest of their bones, and soul's delivery.
Thou art slave to fate, chance, kings, and desperate
    men,
10   And dost with poison, war, and sickness dwell,
And poppy, or charms can make us sleep as well,
And better than thy stroke; why swell'st thou then?
One short sleep past, we wake eternally,
And death shall be no more, Death thou shalt die.

13

What if this present were the world's last night?
Mark in my heart, O soul, where thou dost dwell,
The picture of Christ crucified, and tell
Whether that countenance can thee affright,
Tears in his eyes quench the amazing light,
Blood fills his frowns, which from his pierced head
    fell,
And can that tongue adjudge thee unto hell,
Which prayed forgiveness for his foes' fierce spite?
No, no; but as in my idolatry
10   I said to all my profane mistresses,

Beauty, of pity, foulness only is
A sign of rigour: so I say to thee,
To wicked spirits are horrid shapes assigned,
This beauteous form assures a piteous mind.

14

Batter my heart, three-personed God; for, you
As yet but knock, breathe, shine, and seek to mend;
That I may rise, and stand, o'erthrow me, and bend
Your force, to break, blow, burn, and make me new.
I, like an usurped town, to another due,
Labour to admit you, but oh, to no end,
Reason your viceroy in me, me should defend,
But is captived, and proves weak or untrue,
Yet dearly'I love you, and would be loved fain,
10 But am betrothed unto your enemy,
Divorce me, untie, or break that knot again,
Take me to you, imprison me, for I
Except you enthral me, never shall be free,
Nor ever chaste, except you ravish me.

17

Since she whom I loved hath paid her last debt
To nature, and to hers, and my good is dead,
And her soul early into heaven ravished,
Wholly in heavenly things my mind is set.
Here the admiring her my mind did whet
To seek thee God; so streams do show the head,
But though I have found thee, and thou my thirst
          hast fed,
A holy thirsty dropsy melts me yet.
But why should I beg more love, when as thou

10 Dost woo my soul for hers; offering all thine:
    And dost not only fear lest I allow
    My love to saints and angels, things divine,
    But in thy tender jealousy dost doubt
    Lest the world, flesh, yea Devil put thee out.

19

Oh, to vex me, contraries meet in one:
Inconstancy unnaturally hath begot
A constant habit; that when I would not
I change in vows, and in devotion.
As humorous is my contrition
As my profane love, and as soon forgot:
As riddlingly distempered, cold and hot,
As praying, as mute; as infinite, as none.
I durst not view heaven yesterday; and today

10 In prayers, and flattering speeches I court God:
    Tomorrow I quake with true fear of his rod.
    So my devout fits come and go away
    Like a fantastic ague: save that here
    Those are my best days, when I shake with fear.

Good Friday, 1613. Riding Westward

Let man's soul be a sphere, and then, in this,
The intelligence that moves, devotion is,
And as the other spheres, by being grown
Subject to foreign motions, lose their own,
And being by others hurried every day,
Scarce in a year their natural form obey:
Pleasure or business, so, our souls admit
For their first mover, and are whirled by it.
Hence is't, that I am carried towards the west
10 This day, when my soul's form bends toward the east.
There I should see a sun, by rising set,
And by that setting endless day beget;
But that Christ on this Cross, did rise and fall,
Sin had eternally benighted all.
Yet dare I'almost be glad, I do not see
That spectacle of too much weight for me.
Who sees God's face, that is self life, must die;
What a death were it then to see God die?
It made his own lieutenant Nature shrink,
20 It made his footstool crack, and the sun wink.
Could I behold those hands which span the poles,
And turn all spheres at once, pierced with those holes?
Could I behold that endless height which is
Zenith to us, and to'our antipodes,
Humbled below us? or that blood which is
The seat of all our souls, if not of his,
Made dirt of dust, or that flesh which was worn,
By God, for his apparel, ragged, and torn?
If on these things I durst not look, durst I
30 Upon his miserable mother cast mine eye,
Who was God's partner here, and furnished thus

Half of that sacrifice, which ransomed us?
Though these things, as I ride, be from mine eye,
They are present yet unto my memory,
For that looks towards them; and thou look'st
    towards me,
O Saviour, as thou hang'st upon the tree;
I turn my back to thee, but to receive
Corrections, till thy mercies bid thee leave.
O think me worth thine anger, punish me,
40 Burn off my rusts, and my deformity,
Restore thine image, so much, by thy grace,
That thou mayst know me, and I'll turn my face.

A Hymn to Christ, at the Author's last going into Germany

In what torn ship soever I embark,
That ship shall be my emblem of thy ark;
What sea soever swallow me, that flood
Shall be to me an emblem of thy blood;
Though thou with clouds of anger do disguise
Thy face; yet through that mask I know those eyes,
    Which, though they turn away sometimes,
      They never will despise.

I sacrifice this Island unto thee,
10 And all whom I loved there, and who loved me;
When I have put our seas twixt them and me,
Put thou thy sea betwixt my sins and thee.
As the tree's sap doth seek the root below
In winter, in my winter now I go,
    Where none but thee, th' eternal root
      Of true love I may know.

Nor thou nor thy religion dost control,
The amorousness of an harmonious soul,
But thou wouldst have that love thyself: as thou
20 Art jealous, Lord, so I am jealous now,
Thou lov'st not, till from loving more, thou free
My soul; who ever gives, takes liberty:
     O, if thou car'st not whom I love
      Alas, thou lov'st not me.

Seal then this bill of my divorce to all,
On whom those fainter beams of love did fall;
Marry those loves, which in youth scattered be
On fame, wit, hopes (false mistresses) to thee.
Churches are best for prayer, that have least light:
30 To see God only, I go out of sight:
     And to 'scape stormy days, I choose
      An everlasting night.

Hymn to God my God, in my Sickness

Since I am coming to that holy room,
    Where, with thy choir of saints for evermore,
I shall be made thy music; as I come
    I tune the instrument here at the door,
    And what I must do then, think here before.

Whilst my physicians by their love are grown
    Cosmographers, and I their map, who lie
Flat on this bed, that by them may be shown
    That this is my south-west discovery
10   *Per fretum febris*, by these straits to die,

I joy, that in these straits, I see my west;
    For, though their currents yield return to none,
What shall my west hurt me? As west and east
    In all flat maps (and I am one) are one,
    So death doth touch the resurrection.

Is the Pacific Sea my home? Or are
    The eastern riches? Is Jerusalem?
Anyan, and Magellan, and Gibraltar,
    All straits, and none but straits, are ways to them,
20   Whether where Japhet dwelt, or Cham, or Shem.

We think that Paradise and Calvary,
    Christ's Cross, and Adam's tree, stood in one place;
Look Lord, and find both Adams met in me;
    As the first Adam's sweat surrounds my face,
    May the last Adam's blood my soul embrace.

So, in his purple wrapped receive me Lord,
    By these his thorns give me his other crown;
And as to others' souls I preached thy word,
    Be this my text, my sermon to mine own,
30   Therefore that he may raise the Lord throws down.

A Hymn to God the Father

I
Wilt thou forgive that sin where I begun,
    Which was my sin, though it were done before?
Wilt thou forgive that sin, through which I run,
    And do run still: though still I do deplore?
      When thou hast done, thou hast not done,
        For, I have more.

II
Wilt thou forgive that sin which I have won
    Others to sin? and, made my sin their door?
Wilt thou forgive that sin which I did shun
10   A year, or two: but wallowed in, a score?
      When thou hast done, thou hast not done,
        For I have more.

III
I have a sin of fear, that when I have spun
    My last thread, I shall perish on the shore;
But swear by thy self, that at my death thy son
    Shall shine as he shines now, and heretofore;
      And, having done that, thou hast done,
        I fear no more.

Notes

The Anniversary

The buoyancy and triumph of this poem can be heard and felt in the poem's rhythms. The second verse is something of a problem. Is it more impressive because the playful attitude to time which was present in the first yields to a more serious recognition of the inevitability of death, or is the movement disappointingly flat after the exhilarating quality of the first? The issue of the exact nature of the impact made by the rhythms is intimately connected with the poem's two major preoccupations: the superiority of lovers over common humanity and the relationship between love and time.

1 **favourites** courtiers who are favoured by the King. As in other poems – *The Canonization, The Sun Rising* – the implicit dismissal of the court raises the question of the attitude of the poet to it. Does he reject the court because it is less satisfying than the world of mutual love, or can it be that he creates a compensatory world of mutual love because the court has rejected him?

2 **honours** either judges or privileges.

2 **wits** intellectuals.

7 **no decay** compare this assertion with the impulse to measure love in years (29-30). Is this a contradiction or does the poem create an interesting tension between love in and love beyond time?

9 **running . . . runs** think about how the grammatical distinction between the participle *running* and the verb *runs* helps to establish the difference between permanence and change.

10 **first, last, everlasting day** the first day of creation, the day of judgement and eternity.

11 **corse** corpse.

12 **divorce** are the lovers married or not? If they are, divorce is appropriate, and *two graves* might mean that physical separation in death is the only way their souls could be induced to leave their bodies. If, however, they are not married, the grisly idea of their

souls wanting to remain in the grave with their decaying corpses is avoided, but then is the word *divorce* still applicable?

15   **eyes, and ears** the concentration upon these physical features could show how important the body is to the poet. Does this reduce the effectiveness of 17-20 about souls in heaven? The sadness of parting from the body could be adequately compensated for by placing next to it the idea of the body as the house of the soul with the implied metaphor - *dwells* . . . inmates of the heâvenly mansion as the true home of the soul.

21   **throughly** thoroughly, completely.

23   **earth** this word is crucial for the poem as a whole: it might show that the poet prefers the earthly authority of love in time to a heavenly state, or it might simply mark the point at which the basic confusion of the poem - celebrating love beyond time but ending by celebrating it within time - emerges.

25   **Who is so safe as we?** does this rhetorical question work because the reader sees that lovers are significantly different from kings, or is it bravado trying to counter a real doubt that they might not be safe? A similar question can be asked of *Treason* (26).

27   **True and false fears** what is to be feared – time or unfaithfulness? It is also problematic as to which is the *true* and which the *false* fear.

29   **Years and years unto years** do the rhythms of this line emphasize the glorious character of their noble reign in the kingdom of love, or is there a hint of the grinding repetitiveness of passing years?

30   **threescore** since the span of life is usually said to be threescore years and ten (seventy years), is the idea that the lovers are so superior that their reign lasts longer? If so, is the image of aged lovers disconcerting?

The Apparition

One of the teasing things about this dramatic poem is its tone: is it one of vitriolic rage or that of someone who relishes the grotesque comedy of a ghost succeeding in reaching the girl's bed when the living man did not? The language of crime, guilt and repentance is likewise ambivalent. The problem of tone also touches on the issue of how the poem might be performed: the reader will have to decide whether words such as *When* (1), *Then* (4) (6) and *since my love is spent* (15) should be read with anger or amused playfulness.

3 **solicitation** the act of earnestly requesting or begging something.
5 **vestal** vestal virgins were Roman women who lived chaste lives of dedicated religious service.
6 **taper** candle.
10 **shrink** does this mean more than the act of a tired lover recoiling from a sexually-demanding woman?
11 **aspen** a type of poplar noted for the way its leaves tremble in the wind.
12 **quicksilver** there may be a hint of poison here, as mercury vapour was known to be poisonous.
13 **A verier ghost** even more of a ghost.
15 **and since my love is spent** this seems to contradict the opening line where the poet envisages himself as dead from unrequited love. Is he really in love with her and is saying this in the hope that such a comment may make her submit to him? Is he suppressing his love because his anger is such that he wants revenge? Is he pretending to love so that she may feel guilty? Whatever the answer the inconsistency between (1) and (15) underlines the complexity of the poet's attitude.

The Canonization

This could be said to be a poem of retirement; in that the poet vehemently scorns the public world and opts, instead, for an intimate world of love. (Some scholars have speculated that Donne may have written it in the early years of his marriage, when, due largely to the hostility of his father-in-law, his fortunes were at a low ebb.) (See Approaches p. 143.) Such an interpretation may account for how in the second stanza the poet clearly recognizes how uncertain the world is and yet happily considers its dangers with amused detachment. But if it is about retirement, why does the poem close with the lovers as objects of adoration by *all* (35)? Two further questions are whether, for all its religious language, the poem actually celebrates an entirely earthly love, and whether the poem's changing emotional life – the twists and turns of the poet's feelings – matter more than the poem's argument.

Title   The central conceit of the poem is that the lovers have been *canonized* – declared to be saints – *for love* (36). This could imply that their love had a mysterious and unearthly quality, or that they have been martyred by those who have excluded them from the public world, or that their loving has been so vigorous they have become martyrs by wearing themselves out.

1   This colloquial outburst and many other lines in the poem are remarkable for the abruptness of their speech rhythms. Read the poem out loud to show how its emotional and intellectual life are dependent upon these speech rhythms. Performing the poem may help you to see which are its most crucial words.

2   **palsy** trembling or paralysis.

2   **gout** a disease affecting the joints, commonly associated with old men.

4-9   Are there emotional cross-currents in these lines? The poet might scornfully dismiss the one who disturbs him because he is more than content with loving, or there may be elements of fascination, perhaps even of envy, in the way he quickly scans such worldly concerns as commerce, learning, society and the court. A clue might be found by considering the force of the carefully placed verbs – *Take . . . get . . . Observe . . . Contemplate*: do they suggest purposeful activity that is the envy of the poet or is there something comically mechanical about their frenetic busyness?

6   **Honour . . . Grace** a Lord and a Bishop or Archbishop.

7   **stamped face** a coin bearing the king's head. (The language of economics is a recurring feature of the poem.)

10-18   What is the poet's attitude in this stanza? If there is scorn in his voice, is it still directed at the disturber, or is his real target those Petrarchan love poets who write of lovers' tears drowning the world or their sighs creating storms? (See Approaches pp. 147-8.). Alternatively, is the poet actually revelling in poetic exaggeration?

20   **fly** a moth irresistibly attracted to a candle (*taper*).

21   **die** here, as elsewhere in Donne, there may be a play upon *die* meaning the loss of sexual power after sexual consummation. The traditional idea that sexual intercourse shortens life may also be present.

22-7　The *eagle* is emblematic of masculine sexual initiative and the *dove* of female gentleness and sexual compliance. The *phoenix* is a mythical bird which every thousand years rejuvenated itself by being consumed in flames and rising renewed from its ashes. It was thus emblematic of the resurrection, though here the renewal of sexual power – *we die and rise* (26) – is prominent.

27　**Mysterious** the problem is whether the poem makes us feel that their love is *mysterious* in the sense of its being special and holy. In the stanzas which follow religious language enforces associations of other-worldliness, but can it overcome the impression created in this stanza that their love is sexual athleticism alone? Line 28 raises this problem acutely: if *die* is literal then the religious language which follows might convince us that their love is truly *mysterious*, but what if the sexual connotations of *die* are acknowledged

32　**sonnets . . . rooms** *sonnets* here probably means love lyrics. In Italian, stanza, a unit of verse, means a room. This wordplay raises the question of whether at this point the speaker (or Donne?) is more interested in the nature of writing than he is in the nature of love. Consider, for instance, the force of *Legend* (an inscription), *verse and hymns.*

38　**hermitage** how far should this conceit be pressed? Does it signify their deep mutual understanding or does it point to their sexual union?

40-3　Do these lines mean that the lovers find in each other the essence of all that is valuable in the wider world, or that they possess each other so intensely that they seem to own everything?

45　**pattern** this may recall the Platonic idea (see Approaches p. 145.) of ideal forms towards which the earthly world aspires. This raises the issue of whether the poet wants an earthly or a heavenly love.

The Damp

One way into this poem is to think about 21 – 2, where the poet tells the girl to kill him *as woman* so that he can *die/As a mere man. Kill* and *die* refer to loss of sexual power after consummation. Such plain language raises the issue of whether the poem should be praised for its honest recognition of sexual desire or criticized because in its concentration upon sexuality both the speaker and the girl lose their uniqueness and identity. Closely related is the issue of the second and third stanzas in which a *giant* (11) and an *enchantress* (12) stand for *Disdain* (11) and *Honour* (12), and *witches* (18) for *Constancy* (19) and *Secretness* (19). Giants, enchantresses and witches are all figures from medieval romance; the implication may be that just as the literary forms are old-fashioned, so the moral qualities they represent are outdated. Again, it must be asked: is this a refreshing clearing away of outmoded literary and moral conventions, or does the language erode the nature of love by making it mean little more than sexual desire?

Title   A *damp* is either a noxious fume or a moist, heavy air which depresses or even poisons those who breathe it.

1   **When I am dead** this abrupt monosyllabic opening is echoed by other lines; for instance, *but if you dare be brave* (9). Does it, for instance, suggest annoyance, frustration, the desire to dominate or purposefulness?

3   **cut up** a reading of the line throws a strong stress upon these words. The stresses could either bring out the oddity the poet feels at being an anatomical object, or the poet's hostility towards the mistress.

4   **your picture in my heart** is the tone here one of surprise similar to *The Relic* or is it flattery, implying that her picture in his heart is only what is to be expected?

7   **prefer** promote.

10   **pleasure** the pleasure she takes in her conquests makes her a conventional cruel mistress, delighting in the sufferings she causes. It is, however, important to ask whether, in the poem as a whole, the poet thinks of his pleasure.

13   **Goth and Vandal** the Goths and Vandals were Germanic tribes whose frequent and violent attacks brought about the downfall of the Roman Empire. Their names are traditionally associated with destruction.

16   **Kill** see general note and *The Canonization* (21).

20-4   Do you recoil from the masculine assertiveness of these lines, particularly the demand that the woman exercise her *passive valour* (23), or do you find the lines open and honest in their direct statement of his desires?

24   The idea is that women can perform far longer than men in sexual encounters.

The Dream

A central concern is the relationship between feeling and thought. For instance, the first eight lines seem to issue from the poet's pure delight in his mistress, yet in that delight there is a concern for the branch of philosophy called epistemology – the nature of and the methods used in gaining knowledge. His *dream* is a *theme/For reason* not *for phantasy* (3-4), and she is such as to make *dreams truths* (8). Another aspect of the relationship between thought and feeling is the way the language used to express love is very close to the language of religion. In *cam'st* (18), *rising* (22) and *goest to come* (29) there are both the movements of the girl and the theological pattern of Christ's birth, rising from the dead, ascension into heaven and return at the end of time. Is this extravagant wit, or is it appropriate because both lovers and religious believers praise the objects of their devotion for being her or Himself?

(See Approaches pp. 119-123 for a discussion of the poem's treatment of love and sexuality.)

4   **phantasy** fancy or make-believe rather than reality discovered through *reason*.

7   **true** this may mean faithful and might also, in anticipation of 20, convey the idea that she is wonderfully true to herself.

9-10 Does the poet successfully combine the pleasure and delight he takes in the girl's own self with his desire to make love to her? If there is a natural progression from dreams to *truths* and *fables* to *histories* then the movement from dreaming to acting might be said to be a natural and reasonable one. On the other hand, since the movement he wants is not, as in 8, one within the mind, but from the mind to the body, the request may be jarring.

16   **beyond an angel's art** God, unlike angels, can read the thoughts of the heart. There could be admiration for such a daring piece of wit, surprise at the strangeness of the thought, recoil from its tastelessness, or interest that he wants to use such language of his beloved.

22   **doubt** fear.

26   **fear, shame, honour** you might ask whether, from the girl's viewpoint, *fear* is justified and *shame* inevitable once *honour* is lost.

27 **torches** this image might be considered successful because in line 11 she was a candle (*taper*) and now he is another source of light - a torch. Or is the image merely a bawdy joke on the grounds that candles and torches can function as phallic symbols?

30 **die** a difficult note on which to close a poem. The poet could be playing upon the traditional association of sleep and death, or even, taking up the religious connotations of the poem, drawing a parallel between his *hope* that she will return and the *hope* of the second coming of Christ. A third possibility is a play upon the sexual meaning of *die* – loss of power after sexual consummation.

The Ecstasy

This is one of Donne's most metaphysical poems in the literary sense because conceits are drawn from several branches of learning, and in the philosophical sense (see Approaches pp. 157-161.) because it engages with such metaphysical problems as the union of souls and the relationship between soul and body. Moreover, it tries to fashion a language adequate for souls; the paradox *this dialogue of one* (74) is an example. How successful is, or can, such language be? Does the phrase *soul's language* (22) inevitably imply that something physical must be present - speech (25-6) or a *book* (72) - if that language is to be understood? But perhaps *soul's language* should be understood in another way. The music of the verse - its rhythms and cadences - might be said to be so refined that it sounds like the elevated language a soul might be imagined to use. (See Approaches pp. 150-153.)

In many respects *The Ecstasy* resembles both some of the love and the religious poems, and yet it is worth asking whether it has the ambivalence of attitude that marks the former and the agonizing that is so often present in the latter. Is it the poem's meaning rather than its emotional life that is problematic?

Title An ecstasy is the departure of the soul from the body. Lines 29-48 deal with the ecstatic state, while 49-72 consider the issue, and the significance, of its return. The usual associations of the word - rapture, exaltation, intense delight - do not have to be present in the poem.

1-4 The implications of this stanza, which provides a pastoral setting (see Approaches pp. 147-8) for the lovers, are not easy to focus. Do *pillow* and *pregnant* work sexually, or are you more struck by the visual strangeness of the curving bank? Is the image of the *violet* alluring in that it rests its *reclining head*, or should we bear in mind that when it was written it could be used as an image of modesty and faithfulness? To add to the problem, the lovers modestly sit.

4 **one another's best** each is equally a wooer and a beloved.

5-6 **cemented/With a fast balm** there are several possible meanings here: their hands are joined by their mutual sweat. *Balm* (sweat), according to a contemporary medical idea, keeps bodies from decay. Sweaty palms are a sign of sensuality.

7 **Our eye-beams twisted** sight, it was believed, either came about because the eye transmitted a beam of light on to an object or received one emitted by an object. Is *twisted* wholly in keeping with a stanza about the indissoluble unity of lovers?

10 **all our means** what *means* would make them one? The words might either anticipate the union of souls in the ecstasy or the union of bodies discussed in 49-72.

11 **get** beget. The word might look back to *pregnant* (2) and forward to *propagation* (12) and 37-40 about the transplanted violet. It is important to ask whether such language is metaphoric or literal.

13 **Fate** painters often represented *Fate* as poised above two opposing armies. As with every conceit it is important to ask which implications of *Fate* and *two equal armies* are appropriate and whether other, perhaps less helpful, ones should be suppressed.

18 **We** here the lovers are identified more fully with their bodies than their souls. It is profitable to look at other cases of *we* in this light. Line 51, for instance, is very different.

18 **sepulchral statues** statues on a funeral monument.

21 **refined** made pure. The idea, derived from Alchemy (see Approaches pp. 145-6) is also present in *concoction* (27).

25 **He** why did Donne introduce someone who listens? Does he make the reader feel a member of a small and highly privileged group? Is there the possibility that we should feel the lovers are uncertain

about themselves and so need the assurance of a witness? Is it an instance of the love of display and acting that is present in so many Donne poems?

31   **this** ecstasy.

32   **what did move** what motivated or moved us to act.

34   **Mixture** it was believed that because the soul had so many functions it was made up of a number of elements.

42   **Interinanimates** a mutual infusion of life with a pun on *anima* (Latin for soul).

44   **loneliness** the state of being single.

44   **controls** as in *The Good Morrow* Donne rhymes *controls* with *souls*. The rhyme could be no more than a useful coincidence of sounds or it could reveal Donne's interest in the relationship between love and power.

45   **know** this word might suggest that love in this poem is more a matter of knowledge than emotion. It is worth looking at other poems to see if love is sometimes seen as a matter of reason rather than passions. What, for instance, is the quality of love in *A Valediction: forbidding Mourning?*

47   **atomies** atoms.

48   **no change** since the soul is eternal it cannot change.

48   **invade** the military implications of this word, by reminding the reader of 13-17, raise the issue of whether metaphors and conceits should be restricted to their immediate setting or related to language elsewhere in the poem.

49   What kind of performance best suits this line: one that introduces a conscious element of theatricality or one that reads it as a straight expression of regret?

50   **forbear** avoid.

52   **intelligences . . . sphere** Aristotle taught that each heavenly body consists of a *sphere* governed and moved by a spirit or *intelligence* which inhabits it.

55   **forces, sense** power of bodily movement, the five senses.

56   **dross . . . allay** dross is the waste product of an alchemical experiment: *allay* is an alloy which is of use.

57-8   It is not clear whether Donne is referring to the idea that stars exert their influences by working through the air and/or the notion that angels can only influence people by making bodies out of the air.

62   **Spirits** this term was introduced to try to explain how the body related to the soul.

64   **subtle knot** the connection (*knot*) between body and soul is *subtle*
      in the sense that it is so elusive that it resists description and under-
      standing.

65   **descend** do you appreciate the connection of *descend* and *reach* (67)
      because it suggests a model of mutual attraction and co-operation,
      or are you surprised because the language of the incarnation is being
      used of either the relationship between body and soul or the
      coupling of lovers?

68   Should the prince be interpreted as an imprisoned man or, as some
      have suggested, an unborn child in the womb?

69   It has been suggested that *The Ecstasy* is a poem of seduction. In
      favour is the fact that the needs of the body have been sounded
      since line 49, and here the poet makes a specific proposal. Against
      it is the point that nothing in the poem suggests that, in the sexual
      sense, they are not lovers already. A further point is that the return
      of the souls to the bodies does not mean they are going to make love.
      The meaning of the poem's last line has an important bearing on
      this question.

70   **Weak men** inferior lovers.

The Expiration

This was, in 1609, the first of Donne's poems to be printed. As in a
number of his poems there is an intriguing tension between a
highly-wrought form and the expression of tender feeling: would a
different interpretation emerge if the rhymes (both at the end of
lines and internally) and the contrasts were stressed instead of the
appropriately emotional movement of the poem's lines?

Title   This combines two ideas: the act of a substance being vaporized and
        the breathing away of life at the moment of death.

  4   **happiest day** does this simply mean the happiest time of their life,
        or do the words point to how fleeting their time of love was?

11-12   Does *Except* introduce a clever afterthought which diverts the poet
        both from the sadness of the situation and his beloved, or does the
        emphatic alliteration of *double dead* convey an emotional flatness
        which shows the poet is devastated by the parting?

A Fever

This is a puzzling poem. In the opening and close the language is intimate and tender, whereas in the middle stanzas the writing is philosophically exact (read aloud the fourth stanza), and the beloved is spoken about rather than spoken to. What is to be made of this apparent disparity between feeling and thought? Does emotion govern some stanzas while reason dominates others, or can you see thought in the feeling and vice versa? Another possibility is that feeling is uppermost when the poet writes about his distressing world, but that it recedes when he enters the world of philosophical speculation with its abstractions and unchanging certainties. It might also be that the poet deliberately turns to argument to divert him from the pain of the sick-bed. A complicating factor is the consistent use of a stanza form, which is ideally suited to the incisive expression of arguments. The rhythms (John Carey calls them *impudent*) set up by the stanza give the thought a tightly-packaged feel, which may be at odds not only with the emotion of the situation but also the weighty topics such as death, the end of the world and the nature of the heavens. (See Approaches p. 155.)

1   **die . . . I** what is the effect of this internal rhyme? Does it enforce the pleading sigh of concern with which the poem opens or does it shift attention from the beloved to the poet, so making it a poem in which his distress is greater than hers?

6-7   **this world** in line 7 this *world* means the whole universe, whereas in line 8 it means her body. The linking of the microcosmic – the small world of her body – with the macrocosmic – the large world of the universe – is characteristic of metaphysical writing, but do you think such intellectual ingenuity is emotionally compatible with the situation of a feverish girl and an anxious lover? (See Approaches p. 158-9.)

8   **vapours** evaporates. Donne appears to be fascinated by evaporation; see *The Expiration, Song: Sweetest love* and *A Valediction: forbidding Mourning*. This might be connected with his interest in time and death and/or with his preoccupation with what is material and immaterial, for instance, his treatment of body and soul.

12 **worms . . . worthiest** does the alliteration diminish the world without the beloved (men just become worthy worms) and so stress her importance, or is it a deviation from his concern for her into clever games with words?

13 **wrangling schools** in the middle ages groups (called *schools*) of philosophers debated exactly what kind of fire would burn at the end of the world.

14 **wit** (See Approaches p. 158.)

19 **corruption** contemporary medicine taught that fevers only last so long as there is corrupt or decaying matter in the body. The beloved is therefore an ideal figure, a virtuous beauty.

21-4 **meteors . . . firmament** *meteors* soon burn themselves out because they are part of the changing world below the moon (see A *Valediction: forbidding Mourning* (13)), whereas the *firmament* above is permanent, uncorrupted and therefore unchangeable.

25 **seizing** physical holding and laying a legal claim.

The Flea

The vivid presence of the poet, the way the reader is never allowed to forget the flea, and the remarkable way in which the mistress is present throughout, makes this one of Donne's most dramatically visual poems. But immediacy is only one of its pleasures; unlike some of Donne's poems the argument does not meander but moves carefully, though easily, to its outrageous conclusion. The exaggerated nature of the argument raises the question of whether it should be read as an attempt to persuade an unwilling woman to comply with the poet's desires, or rather as an intricate game (played with the woman or the reader or both?) which should be enjoyed for the engaging subtlety of its strategies. In support of the former view is the way the crucial words *honour* (26) and *yield'st* (26) are significantly held back to the end, but in favour of the latter is the skilful use of contrasts such as innocence/guilt and death/life. Of course, both these features can be used to support the opposite view, as can the exclamations – *alas* (9), *'Tis true* (25) – which can be read as outbursts of feeling or ploys of a skilled debater enjoying his own skill. For those who want to interpret the poem as an attempt at seduction the question of whether the tone is pleading, cajoling, scheming, whining or patronizing is a real one. If you interpret the poem as a game to be enjoyed for itself, you can see the poet deliberately adopting the role of the mock preacher (*Mark but this flea* has the ring of a sermon about it) or the pseudo-scholar who patiently explains a complex matter.

Title   Poems about a lover envying the liberties a flea takes with his beloved's body were popular on the Continent in the sixteenth century. Donne departs from convention by making the flea bite the lover as well as the woman and by presenting the lover as far more restrained than the flea, who *enjoys before it woo(s)* (7).

2   **that** is his reluctance to name what he desires part of a plan to make loss of virginity seem negligible, or is his evasiveness intended to stimulate her desire to yield on the grounds that which is not named but strongly implied becomes alluring?

3   **Me ... thee** does the rhyme enforce the mutual character of the poem, or does the fact that *me* precedes *thee* point to a basic egocentricity?

3   **sucked** it may be that Donne wrote (and intended printers to print) the old fashioned form of s, which resembles f. If such a play (called an orthographic pun) is intended, should it be read as comically indecent, or does it tie in with the lover's strategy by feeding her, in a veiled form, the word which expresses his intention?

4   **mingled** it was believed at the time that the blood of partners was *mingled* in sexual intercourse.

5   **Confess** the position and demanding tone of this word raises the question (a recurring one in Donne) of whether the poet wants to win the girl or the argument. The forceful monosyllables of the conclusion – *when thou yield'st to me* – might suggest the former, but you should also think about this cannot be said (5) and *Yet thou triumph'st, and say'st* (23).

8   **swells** how far should the connotations of this word be pressed beyond its primary meaning of the flea's body swelling with their blood? Can the suggestion of pregnancy (see the first stanza of *The*

Ecstasy), which would surely ruin the lover's strategy, be excluded?

10-11 See Approaches p. 153. The word *three* is important, see note 18.

12-15 See Approaches p. 159.

15 **cloistered** is the poet simply being comic by associating sexual union with the chaste life of the cloister, or should the associations of seclusion and special religious status be taken to indicate, as in *A Valediction: forbidding Mourning*, the self-sufficiency of the world of love and the priesthood of lovers?

15 **living walls of jet** compare *Love's Growth* for another rare example of Donne writing about nature. *Jet* is a black semi-precious stone.

16 **use** her habit of denying him.

18 **sacrilege** there may be a witty parallel in the hyperbole of *sacrilege* between the flea, the man and the woman, and the Holy Trinity of Father, Son and Holy Ghost.

19 **Cruel and sudden** in any performance these words are a test for the kind of interpretation being offered in the reading. The extent to which the anger is assumed will have a bearing upon whether the poem is a game or a serious exercise in wooing.

The Funeral

The central problem of this poem is the matter of tone. The situation is that the mistress has given the poet a lock of her hair but has refused to give herself sexually. Does the poet therefore sadly reflect on his lack of success or is he reproachful or even spiteful? Another possibility is that he is fascinated by the business of burial just as much as he is pained by his failure in love. An interesting feature is the language level; on the one hand the poet enjoys the exaggerated language of martyrdom (dying for one's faith) and idolatry (worshipping idols) and on the other there are very casual phrases such as *Whate'er she meant by it* (17).

Title The poem is about a funeral or, more specifically, the preparation of the body for burial. In Donne's day most bodies were buried in shrouds – tough canvas material which was wrapped round the body and tied at the head and feet. Although there are some similarities between this poem and *The Relic*, the occasion of the latter is not the burial of the body but the opening up of a grave.

1   **harm** one of the things this poem does is mysteriously suggest that the hair is somehow alive. You might like to relate this to the discussion of the *sinewy thread* of his *brain* (9) and the tension, even paradox, of dead and living things.

2   **Nor question much** the effect is that we do question.

3   **hair** the mention of the lock of hair invites a comparison between this poem and *The Relic*.

6   **Viceroy** one who acts in the place of an absent monarch. See *Holy sonnet 14* (7).

6   **which then to heaven being gone** as with other Donne poems, it is important to ask what imaginatively engages the author. Is the poet concerned primarily with the grave, the hair and the woman, or is he speaking lightly of these things because he knows his soul will be safe in heaven?

7   **control** a favourite word of Donne's, see *The Ecstasy* (44).

8   **her provinces** does the admission that his body is subject to the rule of his mistress (a monarch might talk of ruling his or her provinces) flow naturally from the elevated and detailed way he has spoken of the lock of hair, or does it rudely interrupt the line of thought with the uncomfortable reminder that in spite of his persuasive power the mistress is superior to him?

8   **dissolution** consider the way the poem plays on the idea of corruption. He wishes to corrupt her by seduction, yet her hair preserves his body from the corruption of the grave (*dissolution*).

9-11   These lines depend upon a contemporary idea that the body was held together by sinews which ran throughout the body from the brain.

14   **except** unless.

19-20   For a discussion of martyrs and relics, see the notes on the titles of *The Canonization* and *The Relic*.

21-4   The reversal at the close is reminiscent of *Woman's Constancy*. Should the reversal be a complete surprise, or should some of the earlier lines be read in a tone of bitter irony so as to anticipate the poem's ending?

21   **humility** subservience.

23   **bravery** a defiant and rebellious gesture.

24   **bury** the word may have sexual connotations.

The Good Morrow

This poem (an aubade or a poem set in the morning) makes the event of joyfully waking up with a loved one into an image of awakening into a new, adult life of love. This might be implicit in the imagery: since the Renaissance was characterized by voyages of exploration and map making, it may be that the imagery of *sea discoverers, maps* and *worlds* acts as a contrast to the inner, and more authentic, renaissance, or rebirth, of the lovers into mature love.

2   **we** compare the transformation of *thou* and *I* into *we* with the way in which *me* and *thee* becomes *our* in *The Flea*. Are there significant differences in tone between these grammatical changes? (See Approaches p. 148.)

3   **sucked on country pleasures, childishly** it was customary for affluent citizens to send their children into the country to be breast-fed by wet nurses. The possible sexual connotations, such as the pun on *country*, might indicate that in their'childish' state their love was merely physical.

4   **seven sleepers** a legend records that seven Christian youths, who were sealed alive in a cave during persecution by the Emperor Decius, slept for 187 years till they were awakened.

5   **but this** compared to this.

10   **controls** does this word betray a desire in the speaker (in Donne?) to dominate, or could it be a simple acknowledgement that since love is powerful it can control love of lesser things? It could also be that Donne is chiefly concerned to display his verbal dexterity in the witty idea of love controlling love.

13-14   The sense of the argument is: what does it matter even though . .

15   **appears** does the place of this word at the end of the line finally clarify the image of each person's face reflected in the other, or does the word carry with it the suggestion of falseness - appearance rather than reality?

18   **sharp north . . . declining west** *north* is a traditional symbol of coldness and *west* of things in decline. Can the sexual connotations that she will not be cold and his powers will not decline be excluded?

19   According to medieval and Renaissance medicine death occurs

when the elements that make up living things are unequally mixed.
21 **slacken . . . die** should the possible sexual undertones of *slacken* (lose vigour) and *die* (loss of sexual power after sexual consummation) *be acknowledged?* If they are, do they diminish the poem by suggesting that love is merely sexual activity or enrich it through the recognition that sexuality has an important role? A similar issue is encountered in *The Canonization*.

A Jet Ring Sent

This is an unusual poem; it is untypical of Donne in that the poet accepts the conventional attitude of a lover complaining about the cruelty of his mistress, and there is also little sense of intellectual adventure, as the poet sticks with three topics – himself, his mistress and the ring – rather than using them as the starting-point for ingenious speculations. You may find the poem narrow and disappointing; on the other hand, you may prefer its clarity to the wide-ranging scope of the other poems.

Title Jet rings were fashionable and quite cheap. They were often lined with silver and because they could be inscribed they became popular as love tokens. There is some contemporary evidence that they were worn on the thumb.
  1 **Thou** what is to be made of the fact that the poet frequently addresses the ring as *thou* or *thee* and the impression that it is more consistently present to him than is the beloved in many of the other poems. It could be that the poet is addressing his mistress through the ring because he finds it easier to maintain a steady emotional engagement that way than in the turbulence of an actual meeting.
  1 **black** a symbol of constancy because there are no tonal variations in *black*.
  2 **brittle** inconstant, frail and unserious.
  3 **spoke** symbolized. See *Figure* (7).
  5 **Marriage rings** these are usually made of gold and so, unlike jet rings, are *precious* (6) and *tough* (6).

7-8　Is the poet artistically pleased with the way the ring so perfectly figures both their loves or does he regretfully imply that he wishes it was not such an intellectually and emotionally appropriate image?

8-9　**fling me away ... Yet stay** as well as the contrast between *fling* and *stay* there is probably a pun on *jet* which, by derivation from the French *jette* – to throw – was a medieval word meaning to throw or cast away.

Do you think the contrast is too neat and calculated or does it reveal tenderness in the poet, who, because he has been hurt, is sensitive to others – even rings? You may also want to ask whether the pun on *jet* sharpens the situation by making the reader more aware of rejection, or whether such playing with words devalues the emotion.

12　**oh** this could be a conventional poetic way of indicating feeling or it could mark a change from subdued or muted grief to an uncontrolled outburst of anguish.

Lovers' Infiniteness

This poem poses a common problem in Donne: the relationship between feeling and thought. The emotional tone is, at times, that of a puzzled and perhaps even vulnerable man, who is anxious about whether his mistress loves him entirely, and yet much of the poem is in the form of an argument (of a strict mathematical and legalistic character) about whether love can increase and whether he is entitled to all the love he may receive from her. Another feature is that the poem is smoother than those poems in which harsh rhythms express a forthright speaking voice.

Title　Is the infinity of which the poem speaks that of love itself or the lovers?

There is a 1612 setting of a version of this poem by the composer John Dowland.

1　When reading this line aloud you will have to do justice both to the reasoned character of *If* and the (sad? puzzled? despairing?) emotional lilt of the words.

1   **all** the poem's central word: 2, 5, 11, 12, 13 (twice), 22, 23, 24, 33. But is it always used with the same shade of meaning and the same emotional weight?

3-4   In love poetry, particularly of the Petrarchan kind (see Approaches pp. 147-8) lovers sigh and weep. It is important to ask whether Donne accepts the convention or whether there is a degree of ironic undermining.

5   **treasure . . . purchase** the idea of wealth which can be measured out becomes one of the controlling images of the poem. Does he intend the poem to work by playing off the image of love as measurable against the common belief that it cannot be measured? You might also ask whether the idea of measuring love is present in the use of *all*?

8   **bargain** although this word might seem gross and cold-blooded it was used by Elizabethan love poets. For instance, Sir Philip Sidney's *My true love hath my heart and I have his* has this line: *There never was a better bargain driven*.

9   **gift** this word and *gavest* (12) apparently contradict words such as *treasure* (5), *purchase* (5) and *spent* (6). Is this a way of establishing a tension between two ideas of love, or could it be that men pay whereas women give?

16   **stocks** is this meant to contrast unfavourably with the word that applies to his capacity for love – *treasure* (5).

18   **fears** anxieties and doubts. It is worth asking of this and other poems, how safe the lovers in Donne's poem feel. (See Approaches pp. 120-21.)

21   **ground** in law the crops that grow from a patch of purchased land belong to the new owner.

23   Having said he wanted all her love, he now says he does not want it yet. This is a good place to think about the role of anticipation in both Donne's love and religious poetry. How often do the poems look forward to something rather than celebrate its occurrence in the past or present?

31-3 **Changing hearts** could be an echo of the Sir Philip Sidney poem quoted above (8), in which case the poet may be proposing not just pledges of love but marriage. This would be consistent with *so we shall/Be one*. It could, however, be that the poet is only proposing sexual intercourse. The evidence for this is that *liberal* could mean to speak openly about sexual matters.

Love's Alchemy

At whom or what is the anger in this poem directed? It could be a woman or women in general. The insulting coarseness of *centric happiness* (2) and the dismissive closing couplet might support this view. It could also be a poem which scorns love itself, because it has not brought him the joys commonly associated with it. Evidence for this might be found in lines 11-12 on the brevity of sexual pleasure. A third possible object for the anger is the elevated language used by poets and lovers to celebrate love; note, for instance, *Say* (2), *tell* (4) and *swear* (21). A related problem is the actual nature of the anger: is it cynical, bitter, disappointed, resentful, envious or even enjoyably self-dramatizing? In considering these questions think about the contribution of the poem's abrupt rhythms and abrasive sound textures.

Title   Alchemy was a highly complex study, one of the aims of which was to discover, by quasi-chemical means, the philosopher's stone, which would change ordinary metals into gold. As this stone was thought to bestow the power of preservation upon those who possessed it, the title is appropriate: the poet regrets that sexual pleasure is so brief and looks to Alchemy to prolong it. (See Approaches pp. 145-6.)

1-2   Consider the effect of *deeper digged love's mine* and *centric happiness*. Is it the poet's purpose to deflate the elevated claims of lovers by crude sexual joking, or is the reader made uneasy by the strong suggestion of economic exploitation as an analogy of men's sexual enterprises?

3-4   The verbs could express the pride of the sexual athlete and so make the reader recognize him as a man of experience, or they could reduce him to a list of bodily movements carried out in rapid succession in an impersonal and mechanical way.

6   **imposture** a bogus claim.

7   **chemic** alchemist.

8   **pregnant pot** alchemical cauldron in which experiments are prepared.

10   **odoriferous thing, or medicinal** marginally useful by-products of alchemical experiments.

13 **our** the change from the singular to the plural could indicate that the poet is consoling himself by recognizing that he is one of a band of many lovers, or that he has a smaller group in mind, those who see through the silly claims of idealistic lovers.

18 **loving wretch** is the *loving wretch* a lover or a love poet? Given that the poem is a palinode (a poem that contradicts something written in an earlier poem), could it be that Donne is criticizing something that he himself has said in an earlier poem? If so, which poem, or poems, might he have in mind?

22 **spheres** the music made by the revolution of the heavens.

23-24 Is the poet saying that even at their most attractive women are *possessed* by demons, or that even the most engaging women are of no more interest or value than dead flesh (*mummy*) once they have been sexually *possessed*?

Love's Growth

This poem is characteristic of Donne in so far as it starts on a note of puzzlement, which leads to an investigation of the philosophical problem prompted by his surprising experience of love. Conceits are drawn from Alchemy, Astronomy and Medicine, and throughout the pressure may be felt of the traditional conflict between fixed, changeless ideas of perfection and the fact of growth and change. A challenge to the performer is made by the different modes of speech in the poem – the intellectual exactitude (7-14), the nonchalant observation (11-12) which interrupts it, and the sudden appearance (24) of *thee*. Should the poem be delivered as if it were an address to a beloved or to love itself, or a soliloquy from which the poet momentarily awakens in 24?

1 **pure** in Alchemy a substance was *pure* when it was simple and un-changeable.

3 **endure** undergo.

4 **Vicissitude** change, alteration.

4 **grass** grass is a traditional symbol of the decay to which all natural things are subject – *The days of man are as grass, as as flower of the*

field, so he flourisheth. For the wind goeth over it, and it is gone (*Psalm* 103: 15-16). You might ask yourself whether decay as opposed to growth is present anywhere else in the poem, and whether there is a significance either in its presence or its absence.

In 4 the poet has made the discovery (a disturbing or joyful one?) that love is not unchanging but, in the words of the poem, *elemented* (13); that is, part of the changing world of Nature. A useful comparison may be made with those poems, for instance, *The Anniversary* and *The Good Morrow*, in which it is claimed that love does not change and should not alter.

6   **more** the word is an important one in the poem (8, 15).

8   **quintessence** thinkers agreed that the four elements from which all things were made were earth, air, fire and water. Some thinkers speculated that there was a fifth element – *quintessence* – which was supposed to have the power to cure all ills, hence (7). (See Approaches pp. 145-6.)

9   **paining** this could mean causing pain or having an influence upon *soul, or sense.*

10   **working** it was believed that the sun produced warmth, growth and (by implication) a renewal of sexual energy. See also (25).

11-12 These lines are clearly directed at poets (the *Muse* is the source of poetic inspiration). It is interesting to ask whether there is an uneasy relationship between this and other poems by Donne. For instance, in *The Undertaking* love is effectively seen as *pure, and abstract.*

14   **do** the strong implication of physical activity could exclude other meanings of the word *love.*

19-20 Consider the significance of the rare use for Donne of natural imagery: does its presence make vivid the beauty of a changing love, or is the reader inevitably reminded, as in *grass* (4), of how short life and love can be?

20   **awakened root** the phallic implications of this raise the same question as *do* (14).

23   **spheres** the heavens were thought of as a set of spheres, all of which had their centre in the earth - hence *concentric* (24).

A Nocturnal upon S. Lucy's Day, being the shortest day

This poem is a challenge both to the mind and the voice. A reader who wants to appreciate what it is saying about loss, grief and the feelings of nothingness and negativity will have to attend to its rhythms and sounds. (See Approaches pp. 150-153.) Crucial to the whole argument of the poem is the phrase *But I am none* (37), which is the start of the last, and possibly most buoyant, stanza, and yet, as a cadence, one of the flattest and deadest in the poem. This particular problem is an aspect of one of the most interesting tensions in the poem: the placing together of negatives - *privations* (16), *things which are not* (18) - with the much repeated word all and other positive assertions. This raises the question of whether, as a whole, the poem is dark and negative or strangely positive in spite of its subject matter.

Title   Until the calendar was altered in 1752, St Lucy's Day (13 December) was the shortest of the year. The choice of day has prompted speculation that Donne wrote the poem for Lucy, Countess of Bedford, either during a severe illness which she suffered in the winter of 1612/13 or after her death in 1627; other critics argue that the dead beloved must be Donne's wife, Ann, who died in 1617. There is, however, no reason why an actual event must have prompted the poem.

3   **flasks** the stars were thought to store up light originally given out by the sun and so could metaphorically be spoken of as the *flasks* in which gunpowder was kept.

4   **light squibs** the brief flashes and small explosions of a firework.

4   **constant** this clearly contrasts with the brief flashes of the *squibs*, but if it can also be applied to the bereft lover it might mean that without his beloved it is hard to be *constant*.

6   **general balm** either another term for *The world's whole sap* or the preserving substance which, according to some contemporary medical views, prevented decay. Balm also soothes and heals.

6   **hydroptic earth** the earth, like someone suffering from the disease of dropsy, is full of water and yet insatiably thirsty. It is interesting

to speculate why Donne employs this image. See *Elegy 4* (6) and *Holy sonnet 17*.

7   **bed's-feet** it was believed that life ebbs away from a dying man towards his feet; it could also mean that a dying man's life – his interests and concerns – shrinks to the dimensions of the bed upon which he lies.

10   **Study me then** this raises the familiar problem of sincerity or showiness: is this the expression of a genuine awareness that he is in an extreme condition, or is there still an element of self-centred theatricality present?

11   What is the effect of the pace of this line and the positioning of *next world* and *spring*? You might read it as a piece of poetic exaggeration or feel that spring, and all it stands for, really is a long way off.

13   **alchemy** one of the things alchemy searched for was the elixir of life, the essence of life which would cure all ills. Here, however, love produces in him the elixir of death and negativity.

17   The words *ruined* and *re-begot* may function as allusions to the fall of mankind and the salvation, or new birth, brought about by Christ. Are these ideas important in the poem?

21   **limbeck** apparatus used in alchemy to distil (*draw*) substances.

22-7   These lines are apparently in the fashionable Petrarchan mode; that is, they indulge in dramatic exaggeration such as the tears of lovers drowning the world. (See Approaches pp. 147-8.) It is worth asking, however, whether, in the light of the note on line 17, there are also biblical overtones of Creation and Flood. If so, what is their contribution?

28   The fact that *death* is qualified by the remark that the *word wrongs her* indicates that at this point the poem is concerned with the adequacy of words to their subject matter. It is important to look through the whole poem to see if there are other moments when the subject of the poem becomes the poet's difficulty of expressing in words exactly what he is feeling. This question can, of course, be asked of other poems.

29   **first nothing** the state of the world before creation may be hinted at here, because Christian belief insists that the world was made out of *nothing*.

29   **elixir** see note on alchemy (13).

31   **prefer** choose.

33   **Some ends, some means** aims or goals (*ends*), and the ways of achieving them (*means*).

34 **some properties invest** all things that exist have distinguishing characteristics.

37 **nor will my sun renew** is he saying he is so deeply in a spiritual winter that he can expect no spring - no revival of his spirits - or that the sun, the light of life, is identified with his dead beloved?

38 **lesser sun** the real sun.

39 **Goat** the sign of Capricorn which, according to the old Calendar, the sun enters on 12 December. The goat is traditionally associated with *lust* (40).

41 This line is very much a case of how performance affects interpretation. Should it be read self-pityingly, enviously or in a spirit of generous recognition of others' good fortune?

42 **festival** this word introduces a sustained conceit based upon religious ritual – *prepare, hour, vigil, eve*. The poet could be commemorating her and thinking upon himself at the darkest time of the year, or preparing himself to meet her in death.

45 **is** a paradox of this poem is that though it is built on negatives it ends with *is*.

The Relic

This poem resembles *The Canonization* in that both the lovers become objects of religious devotion, and the large claims advanced through the central conceits are ingeniously shown to be appropriate to the earthly love the couples enjoy. Nevertheless, there are differences between the two poems. *The Relic* presents at least two teasing problems: the first is the very strong contrast between the poem's opening with its graphic preoccupation with graves and bones and the completely spiritual love celebrated at its close. The second problem is a familiar one in Donne: the contrast between elevated claims about love and the light movement of the poem – its diverting asides and flippant dismissals.

Title Relics are the bones or belongings of saints, the veneration (honouring) of which was an important aspect of late medieval Catholicism. The Thirty-nine Articles, which set out doctrine for the

Church of England, said that the *Worshipping and Adoration* of relics *is a fond (foolish) thing, vainly invented, and grounded upon no warranty of Scripture, but rather repugnant to the Word of God.* As with the religious poems it is intriguing as to whether Donne is still a Catholic or whether he adopts the Anglican point of view. The word *mis-devotion* (13) suggests that the poem is Anglican, but it is still important to ask whether the imagery shows that his imagination is still Catholic.

1-2　It was a common practice to bury bodies in old graves.

　1　**broke** this word could serve as a foil to the surprising note of courtesy in the second line, or its harshness might indicate the resentment lovers feel at being disturbed in their happy isolation. See *alone* (7).

　3　**woman-head** the primary meaning is the way women behave, but there could also be a play on maidenhead.

　5　**spies** does the poet resent being spied upon, or is there a barely concealed delight in being seen? This problem is also present in *The Canonization* and *The Sun Rising*.

　6　**bracelet of bright hair** a love token of fair hair. Since her hair is the only part of her in the grave, it is surprising that the poet speaks so confidently about a *loving couple* (8).

10-11　The *last busy day* is the Day of Judgement when, at the second coming of Christ, bodies arise from their graves to be re-joined with their souls. *Holy sonnet 7* treats this subject. Does the language used here devalue the idea of the Last Judgement by reducing it to a *busy day*, or does it reveal a touching desire on the part of the poet that, even at the climax of world history, there should be time for lovers to meet? The question depends upon whose view it is. Is it just what the gravedigger thinks, or does the gravedigger rightly see that this was the intention of the lovers?

　12　**fall** occur.

　16　**to make** the issue of the poem's imaginative attitude to lovers and relics is raised here. In the light of the prosaic *he that digs us up* (14) the transformation of lovers into saints might appear ludicrous, but, given that it is *Donne's* idea that the *Bishop and the King* turn them into saints, could it be that he enjoys, and thereby endorses, what they do?

　17　**Mary Magdalen** St Mary Magdalen was a follower of Jesus who, in the imagination of the Church, has become identified with the prostitute, who, in *St Luke's Gospel*, washes Jesus's feet and dries them with her hair. She is usually portrayed as having long, flowing hair.

18 It is difficult to exclude the idea that the poet might be identified with Christ. Such an identification is based on a piece of folklore that Christ and Mary Magdalen were in love. The way the line carries a strong suggestion of a specific identity masquerading beneath a very general description seems out of keeping with suggestions that the poet is either thought to be another saint or one of Mary Magdalen's lovers – a very unlikely candidate for sainthood. The difficulty with identifying the poet with Christ lies in the fact that in the *New Testament* Christ's tomb is *empty*, so there would be no bones in it. It may be that the problem should be looked at from another angle: could it be that the poet jokingly mocks the age of *mis-devotion* for mistaking him for Christ and for thinking that his chaste beloved might be a prostitute?

19 **and some men** the joke is that women are supposed to be more superstitious than men.

21 **paper** poem.

22 **miracles** relics of saints were believed to bring about miracles.

25-6 The belief referred to here is that each person is watched over by his or her own guardian angel. Angels were commonly believed to have no sexual characteristics.

27-8 A kiss of greeting and a kiss when parting was a common practice that implied no sexual interest between people.

29-30 Where does the poem stand over the matter of chastity? Is it saying that it is a *miracle* that the two overcame the impulses of nature to remove the *seals*; that is to say, they resisted the temptation to have sexual intercourse? Another possibility is that *injured* might imply that *late law* has done nature wrong, and that, therefore, the poet is regretting intercourse is prohibited.

32 **pass** surpass.

Song: Go, and catch a falling star

This vigorous and forthright poem (Coleridge said of it:'*Life from crown to sole*') is not obviously elusive or ambiguous. It is, for instance, worth asking just how paradoxical *Things invisible to see* (11) is. A performance of the poem, nevertheless, raises the question of the relationship between the pose of disengaged cynicism on the one hand and its rhythms (could they be described as restless?) and imagery of incessant movement on the other. Such a relationship makes it difficult to decide whether the tone of the poem is one of mocking disbelief at the absurd notion that women could be both beautiful and faithful or a more troubled and even bitter rejection of an idea that has disappointed him.

1-9   The listing of impossible activities could show contempt for the absurdity of there being *a woman true, and fair* (18) or that the poet playfully relishes the prospect of such fantastic exploits.

1   **Go** to whom is this addressed: a would-be lover who believes in female fidelity, a fellow poet or an adventurer who seeks wonders?

1   **falling star** since *falling star(s)* - shooting stars - were thought to be signs of impending disaster, it could be that the impossibility the poet has in mind is controlling fate.

2   **mandrake root** the idea of making a mandrake root, which resembled the human shape, pregnant is absurd in at least two ways: legend has it that when pulled up its scream kills those who hear it, and, in some cases, it resembles the male and not the female form.

4   **the Devil's foot** the devil is commonly represented as having a cloven hoof. To ask who *cleft* it is to engage in an occult version of the highly speculative questions that fascinated medieval theologians, and, in some poems, Donne.

5   **mermaids** *mermaids*, or sirens, were thought to lure sailors on to rocks by their beautiful singing. The line may reveal heroic ambitions: does he want to be like the Greek hero Odysseus who, because be was tied to a mast, heard the sirens yet survived?

8   **wind** a favourable wind for sailors.

9   **honest** this could refer specifically to a true and faithful lover or more generally to the honest person who has no hope of advancement in a corrupt world.

10   **be'est born to** have an inclination to.

10   **strange sights** is it a fault in the poem that neither here nor in *strange wonders* (15) is there an attempt to convey the feel of strangeness or wonder, or is the absence of such feelings appropriate because the *strange sights* do not exist?

18   **true, and fair** do you enjoy this because you see that Donne accepts the convention of the impossibility of beautiful yet faithful women

and concentrates mainly on fashioning the tone of voice that dominates the poem, or do you think the poem is weakened because it unquestioningly accepts this (typically male?) idea?

20 **pilgrimage** in contemporary literature lovers were often spoken of as pilgrims. This word, albeit momentarily, might suggest the possibility that there actually is a *woman true, and fair*, or it could work ironically to undermine such a hope.

20 **sweet** can this be read without irony?

22 **next door** consider the effect of this familiar, domestic term in a poem about heroic tasks and *All strange wonders* (15). It could show the level of his cynicism – he will not even go next door to see a woman who might be *true, and fair* – or the tone could be one of cheerful resignation to a world without such *wonders*.

27 **ere I come** what does he want of the woman who might be *true, and fair*? He might want to admire her as a *wonder*, or court her.

27 **two, or three** does this reveal regret or dismissive cynicism?

Song: Sweetest love, I do not go

In his life of Donne, Isaac Walton claims that this poem, along with *A Valediction: forbidding Mourning*, was written in 1611 shortly before Donne parted from his wife to travel on the Continent.

In some respects the poem is uncharacteristic; there is little philosophizing, and the rhythms of the verse, unlike, for instance, *Go, and catch a falling star*, are smooth and mellifluous. What, however, it shares with other poems is a preoccupation with parting, an anxiety about time and the problem of whether the poet consistently tries to comfort his beloved or becomes distracted by his own ideas.

1-8 See Approaches p. 156.

4 **fitter** is this a compliment or, given *me* at the end of the line, concealed egotism?

8 **feigned deaths** is this moving because it is an ineffectual joke offered in the hope of cheering up his beloved, or is the implication the uncomfortable one that if his deaths are *feigned*, his grief at

parting may also be fake?

11 The sun has neither will (*desire*) nor awareness (*sense*).

13-14 **fear not me/But believe** perhaps an echo of *Fear not, believe only*, *St Luke* 8: 50.

16 **wings and spurs** he could be casting himself in the role of Mercury – the winged messenger of the Greek and Roman gods.

17 **feeble** this marks a decisive change of tone. It could make the poem seem inconsistent or could be read as a sudden sobering up after the poetic flights of fancy in the second stanza.

19 **Cannot add** perhaps an echo of *St Matthew* 6: 27: *Which of you by taking care, is able to add one cubit unto his stature?* Coleridge praised this poem for its *religious thoughtfulness and faith*, possibly because of its awareness, both here and in 17, of human limitation.

21-4 Consider how the structure of the stanza makes these lines different in their effectiveness and significance from the preceding four lines. This question may also be asked of other stanzas in the poem.

23 **teach it art and length** give it cunning (*art*) and allow it scope (*length*).

25-32 When reading this poem aloud particular attention must be given to bringing out the significance of the assonance on *i*. Elsewhere in the poem readers should try to bring out the contribution of the long and short *e* sounds.

26 **sigh'st my soul away** sighing was believed to shorten life.

27 **unkindly kind** should this phrase (an oxymoron or apparent contradiction) be seen as a clever phrase offered by the poet to cheer up his beloved or does its very ingenuity weaken the point that although her tears are natural (*kind*) they might harm him (*unkindly*)?

32 **the best of me** my very self.

33-34 See Approaches p. 156.

33 **divining** foreseeing the future.

36 **fears** are they just her fears?

38 **turned aside to sleep** compare this with the closing three stanzas of *A Valediction: forbidding Mourning*. Do you think a poem about parting is more effective when it uses familiar, domestic details such as the couple turning aside from each other to sleep, or does the strange appropriateness of the compasses conceit get closer to the idea that though apart they are not really parted?

The Sun Rising

Like *The Canonization* this poem opens with an outburst of anger against something which intrudes upon the intimate world of the lovers and like that poem and *The Relic* it closes with the establishment of a relationship between the world of their love and the world at large. Such apparent resemblances, however, need examining; for instance, is the anger of the opening of *The Sun Rising* exactly like that of *The Canonization*? One feature certainly distinguishes this poem: the masculine, possessive pride the lover takes in his beloved. Coleridge responded to this aspect when he wrote: *Fine, vigorous exaltation, both soul and body in full puissance*. The problem of the poem concerns the kind of claim it advances: is the poet making statements as an expression of his joy in possessing his beloved, or should serious consideration be given to the view that he actually believes that their love is so fundamental that it constitutes the basic reality of the world, and that even time and space, both of which are important in the poem, are secondary or even illusory when compared with it?

Title Like *The Good Morrow* the title indicates that this is an aubade, a song sung in the morning.

1 The poet could be adopting the role of the young rebel who derides the older and feebler generation, or might be anticipating stanza three by speaking in an authoritative and even kingly tone.

3 **curtains** probably those round a four-poster bed rather than those at the windows.

5-8 These lines could be contemptuously dismissive of people whose activities are banal, or they could show that the poet finds the activities interesting, purposeful and attractive.

5 **pedantic** in the manner of a schoolmaster.

7 **court-huntsmen** members of the court who hunt or self-seekers who hunt for a position or promotion at court. Both senses could be combined: James I was fond of early morning hunting, so those wishing to curry favour would be up early to join him.

8 **country ants to harvest offices** this probably means hardworking farmers engaged in the jobs associated with harvesting.

9-10   These lines raise a central problem in Donne's verse: the tension between praise of a permanent, unchanging state and a fascination with the variety of the physical world, which is subject to time and change. Does the elevated tone and the measured, majestic pace convince you that an eternal and unchanging state is both superior and desirable, or does the vividness of *rags of time* direct you to the keen pleasures, albeit fleeting ones, that are to be found in the world?

9   **Love, all alike** love, which never changes.

13   **wink** the basic meaning in the seventeenth century was a closing of the eye, though the meaning of a discreet and knowing signal was also available.

14   **her sight** sight of her.

15   **eyes** poets conventionally wrote of the brightness of their beloved's eyes and frequently compared them to the sun.

17   The East Indies produced spices and the West Indies were mined for gold. The images could suggest her alluring richness, or the poet might regard his beloved as an object to be exploited.

20   **hear . . . here** does the echo detract from the majesty of the assertion, or does its playfulness indicate the intellectual superiority of the poet over the sun?

21   The swelling movement of this line could indicate an understandable possessive pride that the lover feels for a beautiful woman, or the image could reveal his desire to control and dominate.

22   **Nothing else is** these emphatic words could be read as exaggeration produced by an extravagant conceit, or a reader might entertain the possibility that the words are not metaphorical but actually insist that the love the couple shares is the only fundamental reality.

23   **play** this word might point to the lesser reality of *Princes*, or it could undermine the lovers' claims by suggesting that it is the lovers who are really *playing*. A similar question is raised by *mimic* (24).

24   **alchemy** dazzling but superficial.

25   **half** since the sun is single he can only be half as happy as the couple.

29   **Shine** the order to *shine* on the lovers is a dramatic change from the opening, where the sun's intrusion was resented. Is this a contradiction which flaws the poem, or can you detect a progression from anger to acceptance?

30   **centre . . . sphere** Donne employs a geocentric rather than a heliocentric picture of the world. (See Approaches pp. 146-7.) Do you find that the change in scientific outlook makes this less

effective, or do the words still appeal to our experience that the sun does indeed appear to move around the earth?

The Triple Fool

In many respects this could be called a light poem: it is humorously directed against the poet himself, its lines are short and some of the rhyming couplets could even be described as snappy. Yet it is important to see that alongside this lightness there is a quite detailed consideration of important matters: how the discipline of art (in this case poetry) controls personal feeling, and how art in performance can awaken in a listener the feelings that inspired the artist. To put it another way: in this poem Donne, or the poet, is both a lover, a poet and a listener. A related issue is the way lines 6-7 convey a very strong sense of the inner life of the poet; the language about subterranean passages – *earth's inward narrow crooked lanes* - suggests the secret depths of the self and the mysterious processes that occur in the mind.

Title The occasion of this poem is the performance in a song of the poet's work. The title invites the reader to see in what ways the poet is a triple fool.

 4 **wiseman** not only someone who is wise but also the person who appears wise in the ways of the world.

 5 **deny** is this weak self-justification or is it a much tougher and more knowing recognition that if he were successful in love even the *wisemen* would envy him?

 6-7 The most popular explanation for why sea water is salty but land water fresh was that land water passed through subterranean passages – *inward narrow crooked lanes* – in which it lost its saltiness.

 10 **numbers** a common term for poetry.

 22 You may feel that the ending is good because it takes up the theme of wise men and fools or that its proverb-like quality is out of keeping with the narrative character of the poem.

Twicknam Garden

Should this poem be performed as the outpourings of a distraught lover or as the expression of a self-consciously dramatic poet who enjoys drawing attention to himself? Both kinds of performance will have to tackle the question of whether there is an ironic edge to any of the words.

Title   Twicknam Park was the home from 1607 of Donne's patroness, Lucy, Countess of Bedford. The garden was elaborately laid out on a symmetrical plan which represented the geocentric image of the universe. (See Approaches pp. 146-7.) Although Lucy's garden did not contain fountains, Donne might have been familiar with them from other formal gardens.

1-5   The changing rhythms of these lines could mark the depth of his anguish, or an element of self-parody might be present.

2   **spring** it is common in poetry to compare and contrast moods with the seasons.

4   **balms** medicinal preparations which soothe and heal.

6   **spider love** it was believed that a spider changed everything it ate into poison.

6   **transubstantiates** the Roman Catholic Church taught that Christ's presence in the Mass was brought about by a change in the substance of the bread, so that although it looked the same its real nature had been transformed. This doctrine was called transubstantiation.

7   **manna to gall** the children of Israel were fed in the desert by the miraculous appearance of a bread-like food called *manna*. Hence in Christian symbolism *manna* is a foreshadowing and sign of the holy communion or mass. *Gall* is a sharp-tasting herb which throughout *The Bible* symbolizes bitter experience.

The significance of this could either be that the word order from line 6 reverses the action of the mass or that the poetic convention that love is a religion is subverted.

9   **True paradise . . . the serpent** according to *Genesis* Adam and Eve were expelled from the Garden of Eden, or *paradise*, because they yielded to *the serpent's* temptation.

10   **wholesomer** better in the sense of more fitting and more appropriate.

11   **Benight** overcome with darkness.

15   **nor yet leave loving** what is to be made of the poet's desire to
continue loving and yet avoid its pain (*senseless* means without
sensation)? Does it successfully show a man in the paradoxical state
of hating the pain of love yet longing to continue loving, or does it
show that the poet is interested in strange and extreme states?

17   **mandrake** a plant which was supposed to scream when uprooted.
See *Song: Go, and catch a falling star* (2).

19-25   What is the relationship between the poet's emotions and the
imagery? Are his feelings momentarily allayed by the ingenuity of
the fountain image before they break out in *Alas, hearts . . .*, or is that
outburst as staged as the image (a comic one?) of lovers tasting their
mistress's tears?

19   **vials** tear-vessels.

20   **love's wine** possibly a reference to the mass.

27-8   Does the poem close with an anguished image of the poet's
misfortune in loving a woman who, unlike all others, is faithful to
someone else, or is there a hint of comedy in the absurd situation
of loving the one woman who will remain faithful?

The Undertaking

In this poem there is a puzzling tension between the elevated subject
and the poem's form and tone. The poem celebrates *loveliness within*
(13) and yet it is written in a brisk metre, and its tone is proud,
boasting and perhaps even smugly self-satisfied. A further aspect of
this tension is the refined character of the love on the one hand and
the terse, philosophical argument on the other. These disparities
were noted by Coleridge, who wrote: *A grand poem; and yet the tone,
the riddle character, is painfully below the dignity of the main thought.* See
Approaches p. 157.

Title   An alternative title is 'Platonic Love'. Platonism (thought that
derived from the Greek philosopher Plato) taught that the world is

only a dim reflection of the real world, which exists in an eternal and unchangeable form. Given that view, the highest kind of love is that which ignores the body and seeks to love the mind because it is more akin to the eternal and unchanging world. The contrast between the material world and the real world is present in a number of Donne's poems.

1 **braver** finer, more glorious and more impressive.

2 **Worthies** the Worthies were a group of nine heroic figures who exemplified all the qualities of ideal warriors. In public pageants they were represented by men who loudly boasted about their marvellous deeds.

4 **hid** it is unusual to find a poem celebrating secrecy when so many of Donne's poems are showy and theatrical. Does the poet keep his secret hidden?

5-8 See Approaches p. 153.

6 **specular stone** a transparent stone used in building ancient temples. Since Donne and his contemporaries believed that it was no longer available, there was no point in learning the very difficult art of cutting it.

8 **cut** here and elsewhere in the poem a reader must do justice to the way some words have a very incisive stress.

14/16 **loathes/oldest clothes** do you think the poet finds it easy to dismiss *colour* and *skin* as *clothes*, which are to be loathed? You might also ask whether the insistence of the rhyme creates the impression that inner loveliness matters more than the flesh.

17 **as I have** see *Twicknam Garden* (19-22) for another view of the poet as a pattern of true love.

18 **Virtue attired** if you have decided that *oldest clothes* make the flesh faded and uninteresting, is it possible to respond positively to the image of *Virtue* clothed in a *woman*?

19 **say** is there the implication that the real achievement lies not in loving but in saying?

20 **the He and She** given that the sentence of which this is the climax starts with a questioning *If*, is there a hint that the poet acknowledges that it is very difficult to ignore sexuality?

22 **profane men** poets often spoke of love as a religion and of ordinary people as irreligious or *profane*.

A Valediction: forbidding Mourning

If Isaac Walton is right in saying that this poem was written by Donne when he parted from his wife for a journey to France in 1611, the *I* of the poem may be the poet himself. If, however, this is a guess, both the *I* and *thou* could be fictional. Would this make a difference?

The relationship between reason and emotion in this poem is particularly enigmatic: is it an argument touched by emotion, or a lovingly intimate poem that controls feeling by expressing it in the form of an argument?

1-8   See Approaches pp. 125-6.

  1   **As** this word often introduces an argument: could it also introduce a more emotional kind of speech?

  1   **virtuous men** those with a clear conscience die peacefully.

  5   **melt** think about the force of this word in the light of its common meaning in Donne's day of yielding to an emotion or giving way to tears. Consider, also, its importance in the poem in relation to the plea for *firmness* (35).

  11   **trepidation** the system of astronomy originated by Ptolemy (See Approaches p. 144.) held that the spheres surrounding the earth trembled as they revolved; this affected the motion of the planets but was neither felt nor caused damage on earth. It was, thus, *innocent* (12); that is to say, harmless.

  13   **Dull sublunary lovers** since the fall ruined the region below the moon, earthly lovers are tarnished. (See Approaches p. 145.)

  14   **(Whose soul is sense)** the dullness of *sublunary*, or fallen, lovers is evident in the fact that their affections originate from, and are entirely controlled by, the senses.

  17   **refined** purified.

  20   **Care less** what force do these words have, given that the poet lingers over *eyes, lips, and hands* before coming to the word *miss*?

  24   **aery thinness beat** gold beaten to a near transparent state to produce gold leaf.

25-36   In Donne's day compasses performed the tasks now carried out by both dividers and compasses. Are three uses present here - measuring or dividing the distance between two points; the opening and subsequent closing of the compasses in the course of taking a measurement; the drawing of a circle?

The precision and detail of this conceit provokes a number of questions. Does the detail enhance or detract from the poem as a whole? Is the precision an embodiment of the firm control of emotion for which the poet so beguilingly pleads, or is the conceit too cold and austere? Is the attention necessary to appreciate the conceit out of proportion to the space it occupies in the poem?

36 **end, where I begun** is the image of a circle being completed less satisfactory as a symbol of homecoming than the closing of compasses (29-36)?

Woman's Constancy

Is this poem a game played between poet, mistress and reader, or do you find in it the expression of a real emotional state in which attraction coexists with an impulse to mock and ridicule? Your answer to this question could be given in a performance of the poem. If you attempt to sort out the problem this way, the way *whole* (1), *now* (4), *just* (5), *any* (7) and *but* (10) are said will be crucial.

Title How applicable is the title?

2 **when thou leav'st** is the tone here one of sad resignation in the face of female infidelity, or can you detect the deliberate adoption of the pose of a hurt man?

2 **say** it is important to ask whether this is a case of the real subject matter being not what people do but the words they use.

3 **antedate** to assign an earlier date to an event or agreement.

4-13 Do the four sentences beginning with *Or* suggest the lady's remarkable capacity for argument, the poet's bitter realization of just how fickle the lady is, or are they arguments the man puts into the lady's mouth in order to prepare for the reversal with which the poem ends?

10 **sleep, death's image** it was a poetic convention to write of sleep as being akin to death.

14 **lunatic** the mistress could be a lunatic because she foolishly wants to abandon her lover or because, like the moon, she is changeable.

14 **'scapes** tricks or wiles often prompted by sexual motives.

15 **Dispute, and conquer** do these words reveal the basic attitude of the lover towards his mistress, or is their aggressively masculine edge blunted by the nonchalant and even indifferent tone of the couplet in which they appear? (See Approaches p. 125.)

16 **abstain** are you surprised by his refusal to tackle the arguments of his fickle mistress or do you sympathize with his reluctance because the many arguments in the poem only show how unreliable the words of lovers are?

Elegy 4: The Perfume

The dramatic situation of this poem is akin to a domestic comedy: a young man is courting a girl, who seems willing enough to return his love but is locked up by a jealous family. The reversal of the young man's plans comes about ironically; although he has evaded the father, mother, children and even the grim serving-man he is given away by his *loud perfume* (41). Such a situation gives Donne the opportunity of creating a distinctive voice (the rough couplets are crucial here) yet, as with other poems, there are moments when psychological integrity is threatened by the author's interest in arguments and ideas.

2 **escapes** adventurous escapades of an amorous nature.

3-6 Is the tone simply one of hurt outrage, or is there also pride and even enjoyment in being singled out as the object of her father's anger? The use of *traitorous* (5) and the spite of *hydroptic* (6) (suffering from dropsy) suggest that the tone is one of outrage, but the positioning of *So am I* (5) may indicate his pleasure at being the centre of interest.

3 **at bar** in a criminal court the accused stands at the bar.

7-8 The *cockatrice* or basilisk is a kind of lizard which was believed to kill by its looks. The meaning here could be that her father is so fierce that he can even kill a cockatrice, or that his eyes are so old and his vision so bleary (*glazed* could have that meaning) that spying on the lovers is as likely to be as successful as trying to outstare a cockatrice.

11 **Hope of his goods** the young man could be accusing the father of

only being interested in his daughter's price on the marriage market, or the lover could be quoting the father's view that it is the lover who is interested in her riches. You might also ask yourself whether the personality of the lover inclines you to think of him as a trustworthy man motivated by love or as a daring opportunist out for sexual pleasure.

14 **buried in her bed** a play on the traditional association between the grave and the bed.

18 **rings . . . armlets** love tokens.

20 **swoll'n** pregnant. See discussion of *The Flea* (8).

21-2 The mother is closely watching her daughter for signs of pregnancy such as a pale complexion or a sudden liking for a particular food.

23 **politicly** scheming with the ulterior motive of securing a confession of guilt from her daughter.

25-26 What meaning is given to *love* by this couplet? Does the thought that *love* led her to *gull* (deceive or cheat the unwary) narrow the range of the word so that it means little more than a selfish desire to achieve one's own ends, or does the idea of the younger generation outmanoeuvring the older give it an attractive and adventurous quality?

29 **ingled** dandled or fondled by their father.

34 **Rhodian Colossus** the Colossus of Rhodes (one of the seven wonders of the ancient world) was an enormous statue that was said to stand across the entrance to Rhodes harbour.

41 **loud** look through the poem for words that are a contrast to *loud*.

47-9 The *isle* of Britain, where the native beasts are cattle and dogs rather than the exotic *unicorn*.

52 **oppressed** this probably refers to pressing prisoners with heavy weights to make them talk.

53-70 How should we understand this attack upon perfume? The survey of how perfume is used and the deft concluding couplet (69-70) might enforce the poet's anger because it shows him summoning all his intellectual powers, or the focus of interest could be the intricacy of the argument and the dramatic expression of his plight.

57 **Base excrement** it was a popular joke that perfume was merely the excretion of flowers and animals.

59 **silly amorous** a foolish lover.

64 **substantial** the real, solid things which those in a Prince's court overlook because they are distracted by empty fashion.

67-8 **simply . . . joined** things made up of loathsome separate (*simply*) entities are no better when made into a compound (*joined*).

70 **rare** good things are universal not unusual (*rare*) as is perfume.

71-2 Is the close of the poem successful? The argument against is that the final couplet is an afterthought, which reintroduces the now almost forgotten situation of the lover being frustrated by the father. The argument in its favour is that it returns the reader to the opening concerns of the poem and provides a new use for the perfume.

72 **corse** corpse.

Elegy 5: His Picture

This is a poem of parting which depends upon some of the conventions of contemporary poetry: parted lovers were often written of as *dead* (3), and those united in deep love customarily spoke of themselves as superior to *rival fools* (11) – ordinary people. What distinguishes this poem, however, is its blend of vivid physical detail and quasi-theological argument. As so often in Donne, it is the balance or tension of these elements that gives the poem its life.

1 **picture** miniature portraits, often no wider than 4 to 5 centimetres, were commonly given as parting gifts.

3 **dead** can this be read both metaphorically and literally?

4 **shadows** a picture could be spoken of as a shadow. A ghost or shade could also be called a shadow.

5-10 Do these lines act as a foil to show how mature the beloved's love must be to ignore his battered appearance, or does the very physicality of the lines impress the reader more than the arguments in the latter half of the poem? The latter would make the presentation of possible disaster more interesting, and even more convincing, than the love that can look beyond appearances to the inner self.

10 **powder** gunpowder.

13 **This** the portrait.

13 **and thou shalt say** how convincing is this? Does he have complete confidence in the maturity of her love and so can predict how she will react, or is he aware of how repulsive he might be and so is leading her to respond in a way which is favourable to him?

18   **milk** in *The Bible* and in much religious literature it is common to draw a distinction between the spiritually young who, like babies, need milk and the mature who can feed on the real meat of religion. For instance: *I gave you milk to drink, and not meat*, 1 Corinthians 3: 1.

Elegy 16: On his Mistress

The dramatic situation of this poem may be compared to *Elegy 4*. In *Elegy 4* the plot resembled a domestic comedy, while here the beloved's wish to accompany the poet makes her more like the heroine of a romantic, even a Shakespearean, comedy, who disguises herself in order to be with the man she loves. It is interesting, also, to explore the differences: in *Elegy 4* the poet accepts the role of the lover, whereas in *Elegy 16* the poet persuades his beloved not to adopt the role of the disguised heroine. You may ask yourself whether or not this is significant. It is a highly wrought piece with many repetitions and carefully paced climaxes, yet, as with many Donne poems, such an elaborate patterning in the language exists alongside what seems to be genuine feeling; note, for instance, the touching simplicity of the close.

1   **fatal** this word could point to the depth of their love by implying that even at their first meeting (*interview*) they were destined for each other, or it could anticipate the fears of his death, which are the subject of lines 50-4.

3   **remorse** the tenderness and pity she feels for him.

4   **my words' masculine persuasive force** these words could imply an understanding of how the beloved will react to him, a self-centred celebration of his prowess in loving, or, given *words'*, a comment upon the power of his poetry.

7   **calmly** should the poet be believed when he says he begs *calmly?*

8   **want and divorcement** her absence from him due to separation.

11   **overswear** swears oaths of constant love again and again.

14   How do you respond to this request? Bearing in mind the firmness of line 12, do you see the poet as expressing an admirable care for his beloved by shielding her from danger and giving her the dignity

of a *true mistress*? Alternatively, you might see her desire to disguise herself as a *feigned page* as brave and enterprising, and his desire to keep her at home as a (perhaps unconscious) resort to the narrow stereotype of woman as passive and domestic compared with active and adventurous man.

16   **only** bearing in mind the problem posed above, does this word mean she is the only one who is worthy or her only worthiness lies in her ability to raise in him the thirst to return?

19   **move** remove.

21-3   Donne appears to be recasting a Greek myth here: instead of *Boreas* (21) - the north wind - carrying away a girl called *Orithea* (23), he makes *Orithea* a tree or plant which, is *in pieces shivered* (22) by *Boreas*.

24   **proved** undergone or suffered.

25   **unurged** without compulsion or necessity.

27   **Dissemble nothing** the immediate meaning is do not disguise yourself. Can, however, the idea of deception be excluded?

28   **strange** to be either a stranger or to be someone whose identity is concealed. *Strange* has appeared in line 1. Is there a significant link between the two lines?

30   This line can be usefully compared with line 4. Is the comparison only relevant to this poem, or are similar attitudes to the characters of men and women found in other poems?

31   **apes** fools. The point of comparison is based on the proverb that apes are still apes even if they are richly dressed.

33   **chameleons** in the same way that chameleons change their colour so the French change their moods. There may be the implication of untrustworthiness.

34   **Spitals of diseases** a *spital* is a hospital which treated venereal diseases.

35   **Love's fuellers** those who stoke up their own passions.

36   **players** the poet criticizes the French for being *players*, but can you exclude the idea that he is thinking of his beloved as a player and that he is something of one himself?

37   **know** does the poet successfully play upon the two meanings of *know* – recognize and have sexual intercourse with? The linguistic playfulness might seem distracting and/or trivial in the face of the threat posed by the French.

38   **indifferent** oblivious as to whether his lust is satisfied by either man or woman.

41 **Lot** in *Genesis* 19: 4–11 the men of Sodom are so aroused by two angels who visit Lot that they demand he hand them over so they can satisfy their lust.

42 **spongy hydroptic** see *A Nocturnal upon S. Lucy's Day, being the shortest day* (6).

43-6 A *gallery* (44) is a long room, often found in palaces or mansions, which adjoined the main room of the house. If the King were present, those wishing to see him would have to wait in the gallery. How does the image work? It could be a kind of allegory in which the soul waits to be called into God's presence or it could show life in England to be attractive in comparison with the moral squalor of the Continent.

47 Compare this with the last stanza of *Song: Sweetest love*.

51-4 How should this outburst be understood? Does it show he knows her so well he understands her fears, or does a phrase such as the *white Alps alone* (53) indicate he finds the prospect of travel exciting?

55 **Augur** forecast or predict.

55 **except** unless.

55 **dread Jove** God, but perhaps with a hint of the wilfulness and un-predictability associated with Greek and Roman Gods.

Elegy 19: To his Mistress Going to Bed

This poem openly deals with love-making, is physically graphic and its word-play is frankly, and sometimes unsubtly, sexual in charac-ter. Nevertheless, there are puzzling elements: religious lanuage is strongly present (its effect is one of the challenges to the reader), the mind of the poet is sometimes as engaged as his body (the discourse on the nature of nakedness (33-43) is intellectually quite complex) and, for all its specificity, it is not clear what kind of sexual encounter is taking place. Could it be the consummation of a marriage, the love-making of a married couple, the seduction of a high-class woman or a casual, though very amorous, escapade in a brothel? This uncertainty raises the joint problems of its value and success: should readers pay little attention to the question of the poem's situation and enjoy the sensual pleasures (and joys?) of the poet's account of his anticipated love-making, or should they follow up the varying (and perhaps contradictory) implications of the imagery and so find the poem a forceful though confused and unsatisfactory composition?

1 **Come** many poems which are invitations to love either start with or emphasize this word.

1 **my** to what extent is the character of the whole poem indicated by so prominent a use of the personal pronoun *my*? What is the effect of the internal rhymes *my ... defy ... I ... I ... lie*? Are they assertive or are they close to the similar but distinctly sighing sounds of the fourth stanza of *Sweetest love*?

2 **labour ... in labour lie** the first *labour* means sexual activity, the second agonized anticipation.

3 **The foe** military language was often used in love poems. Is such language merely playful or does it hint at an emotional conflict? The sexual joking of much of the poem might point to the former possibility, while the grammar (the poet gives orders) may lend support to the latter view.

4 **standing** here and in lines 11-12 and 23-4 the poet calls attention to his erect penis. Should such references be read as necessary to the creation of an erotic atmosphere, or, given the unease about sustaining an erection (*tired*) should the poem be read not as the expression of the confident and skilful lover who takes his time over loving but an anxious and possibly self-doubting man who almost forces his beloved into complying with his desires?

5 **heaven's zone** the Milky Way.

6 **a far fairer world** this is the first time in the poem that a woman's body is seen as a world. Readers should try to be aware of the idea's implications: does it signify how wonderful she is or his desire to discover, exploit and conquer?

7 **spangled breastplate** ladies often wore jewelled stomachers, which covered their breasts.

9 **harmonious chime** either the jingling of the jewels or her chiming watch.

11 **busk** corset.

15 **wiry coronet** a decorative band of metal worn round the brow.

16 **hairy diadem** since diadems were associated with royalty the implication may be that her natural beauty, in this case her hair, exceeds the beauty of her *coronet* (15). How important is this idea in the poem as a whole?

17-18   The placing together of removing shoes and the bed as *love's hallowed temple* may be intended to prompt the religious idea of taking off shoes in a holy place. If the idea is valid it raises the issue of whether the religious language of the poem is clever word-play or an indication that the poet does feel his beloved to be special and their sexual union a holy act. Consider Wilbur Sanders' view that this poem *stands nearer to religion than all the conscious spirituality of The Ecstasy*.

21   **Mahomet's paradise** Donne follows the popular view that Moslems imagined that in paradise there was endless sexual pleasure.

22   **Ill spirits walk in white** Donne's contemporaries believed that it was often exceedingly difficult to tell a good from an evil spirit, because evil spirits were often disguised as good ones, that is, they appeared in angelic white.

23   **sprite** spirit.

24   **hairs . . . flesh** given the difficulty of distinguishing between good and evil spirits, should this line be read as a simple and entertainingly bawdy solution to the problem, or, given the implication of the angelic purity of the woman, is the concentration on the poet's erection a distracting and disappointing crudity?

25   **Licence** allow, but possibly also the idea of taking out a licence for mining or other kinds of economic exploitation.

27   Different parts of America were described as new-found lands.

29   **empery** empire.

30   **discovering** uncovering.

31   **bonds** her loving arms that will hold him fast, a legal agreement or, even, the *bonds* of indissoluble marriage.

32   **seal** this usually refers to the sexual organs, as in *The Relic* (29 – 30). The word also refers to the sealing of a legal document.

34-5   Does this comparison work? Is it a contradiction to praise naked bodies by comparing them to souls *without* bodies, or is it successful because it brings out a kind of religious wonder the poet feels in the presence of his naked mistress?

35-8   Donne alters the story of Hippomenes, who distracted Atalanta in a race by throwing golden balls in her way, by making Atalanta the one who distracted men by throwing down jewels. The lines leave it unclear as to who exactly is the fool.

40   **laymen** the idea here is that ordinary men (*laymen*) need pictures or fine bindings whereas real scholars do not.

41-3   True lovers are only allowed to see the nakedness of women if women dignify their lovers with that privilege. In this they are like those elect (and hence small in number) believers who are counted righteous (*imputed*) by God and so can understand the revelations of *The Bible* (*mystic books*). Should this elaborate conceit be welcomed because it elevates the position of the woman, or should it be criticized because *revealed* presents too great a disparity in meaning between religious illumination and the sight of sexual organs?

44 **midwife** is the word suitable? For a similar problem, see *The Flea* (8).

46 **penance . . . innocence** the implication is that although she wears white she is neither penitent (those guilty of sexual crimes did public penance in white garments) nor innocent of sexual experience. Is the line incompatible with *these angels* (23)?

48 **covering** the difficulty here is that this word was customarily used of the copulation of horses and not people.

Holy sonnet 6

In the octave of this sonnet (1-8) the poet creates in detail the intense musings of a man anticipating his own death, and in the cooler and more theological sestet (9-14) he attempts to calm the fears aroused by the opening through the consoling hope of imputed righteousness. Such a clear division between octave and sestet inevitably raises the problem of whether one section is more effective than the other: is the octave finer because of its vivid imagery and high emotional temperature, or should a reader be more impressed by the intellectual clarity of the sestet and find it more appropriately humble and self-aware than the heated, theatrical rhetoric of the first section?

1-4 Why does the poet rapidly move from one image to another? Is such mental agility the expression of a fascination with death, or is he so gripped by fear that he desperately seeks to control the unknown by portraying it to himself in a series of vivid and familiar images? A third possibility is that he is dramatizing his own plight in order to alert, even pressurize, readers into recognizing the seriousness of the poem's subject matter.

5 **gluttonous death** what is the effect of imagining death as a hungry thing which, at the very moment of the poet's passing, will *instantly unjoint* body and soul? Should readers recoil in horror from a predatory but otherwise hardly focused creature, or do the words *gluttonous* and *unjoint* render death grotesquely comical by reducing it to a glutton or butcher? If the former, is the effect consistent with the calm of *and I shall sleep a space* (6) and if the latter, does the poem suffer or benefit from such black humour?

7 **that face** what face? Does the fact that there are a number of answers – God, death, the devil – enrich the poem by highlighting the poet's fear and uncertainty, or diminish it by making the fear vague?

13 **Impute me righteous** this essentially Anglican rather than Roman Catholic cry for help derives its force from the doctrine that since Adam's sin, due to the fall, is attributed, or imputed, to all, salvation is only possible if people are correspondingly imputed righteous by the merits of Christ's suffering and death upon the cross. The sermon in the second *Book of Homilies* (1563) that explains Article XI on justification contains this remark: *we cannot be accounted righteous, but by Christ's merits imputed to us*.

14 **For thus I leave** in what state does he leave the world? Does the dramatic gesture implicit in *thus* point to his fallen or redeemed state? The words *the world, the flesh, and devil* do not resolve the ambiguity: they are a reference to the Baptism Service in *The Book of Common Prayer* but they could equally mean that, as at baptism, the poet has renounced them or that, since he is still polluted, he draws attention to this in order to strengthen his plea for mercy uttered in the previous line. The significance of the theatrical close (it is like an actor's dramatic exit) depends upon which interpretation is adopted. Does the poet confidently depart knowing he has been imputed righteous, or is the histrionic gesture an indication of just how self-regarding the poet is and, consequently, of how great, in the reader's eyes, is his need for mercy?

Holy sonnet 7

The design of this sonnet sets up striking contrasts between the octave and the sestet. (See Approaches pp. 141-2.) For instance, what is to be made of the way the colourful, highly peopled and even theatrical opening is followed by a visually spare and highly individualistic close? The overall stance of the poet is puzzling: in the octave he speaks in bold imperatives, while in the sestet he is fittingly humble.

See Approaches p. 130.

1 **round earth's imagined corners** what is the effect of coupling *round* and *corners*, and what does *imagined* contribute? The words could make readers aware of how the poem is crafted and so distance us from its substance, or the potentially paradoxical character of the language could form a fitting preparation for a poem about an event so unparalleled that words have to be stretched and extended beyond their ordinary meanings in order to imagine it.

4 **to your scattered bodies go** at the last Judgement souls will be reunited with their bodies.

5 *The flood* refers to Genesis 6-8 (the first book in *The Bible*) and *the fire* to *Revelation* 8 (the last book in *The Bible*). What contribution does this time span – from the beginning to the end – make?

6 **agues** diseases.

9 **But let them sleep, Lord** this could be the impudently blasphemous request (demand?) of a grossly egocentric man, or there could be an uncertain humour about the words that draws attention to the gulf between the poet and Christ.

10 **abound** in *Romans* 5: 20 St Paul writes: *where sin abounded, there grace abounded much more*

12 **there; here** does this simple placing together enhance or detract from the gravity of the sonnet?

13-14 Is the tone of the close assured or anxious? The almost colloquial *for that's as good* might indicate confidence or nervous bluster. Likewise, Christian doctrine asserts that Christ has sealed everybody's pardon with the blood of the cross, yet the effect of *As if* might make the final line sound more tentative.

See Approaches p. 130.

Holy sonnet 10

The constantly changing moods of this sonnet may be read as a kind of poetic duel with death; the poet's word-play corresponding to skilful swordsmanship, and the variations in pace and emotional intensity to the thrusts and parries of the poet's attack and defence. Because of these changes it is difficult to characterize the overall tone: is he serious in the face of a mighty foe, cosily intimate and even casually witty at death's expense or denigrating almost to the extent of being sneering? Another problem is that the argument is clearly false, being based on analogies such as the conventional one between sleep and death. A defence of this is that the poem is explicitly about the *language* we use to speak of death - *though some have called thee* (1) - in which case what the poet does is playfully exploit some of the ways in which people speak of death in order to belittle the kind of talk that calls it *mighty and dreadful*. Another defence is that what matters is not the argument itself but the creation of an anxious mind that seeks to control the terrible threat of death by bracing itself with as many images as it can. Such a defence proposes that the poem is to be valued for the anguish evident in the variety of imagery rather than for its reasoning.

1   **proud** the word has the sense of being impressive and awe-inspiring as well as the standard meaning of boastful self-confidence. Both senses are also present in *swell'st* (12).

4   **nor yet canst thou kill me** the quickened pace of these heavily stressed monosyllables might suggest a lively confidence that the poet has the measure of his opponent, or they could be a defensive thrust at a strong adversary whom he fears.

8   **delivery** the soul is delivered in the sense that at death it is born into eternity and also in the sense that it is delivered from the prison of life.

13   **wake eternally** God is not directly mentioned here or anywhere in the poem. Does this mean that the poet feels death to be more immediate than God, or is there a quiet confidence in the restraint of the language that is more appealing and religiously profound than the direct appeals of, for instance, *Holy sonnet 14*?

14   **Death thou shalt die** is this an effective end to the poem? It might

be thought inconsistent for the poet to have written off the fear of death throughout the poem and then serve it up as a threat to Death itself at the climax. But that view might miss the point that Death is only terrible within the world, for, paradoxically, when people die they leave Death's realm and so to them Death is dead.

Holy sonnet 13

The tension in so many Donne poems between divine and earthly love is vividly present here. The octave is intensely and vividly detailed in its presentation of the crucified Christ. Here (and in other of the Holy sonnets) Donne may be dependent upon traditions of religious meditation in which those who prayed pictured in their imaginations scenes from *The Bible*. By contrast the sestet is more relaxed and even casual. You can picture the poet confidently shaking his head in *No, no; but as in my idolatry* (9). As with most of the sonnets, it is important to see how the close settles the intellectual and emotional energies.

2　**Mark** the word had contemplative and meditative connotations.

4　**countenance** in *The Bible* this word is frequently used of God's face. *The Lord lift up his countenance upon thee (Numbers 6-26)*.
(It is interesting to think about how Donne writes about the face of God and the face of his beloveds.)

5　**amazing** frightening or even horrifying.

6　**pierced head**: see *St Mark* 15: 17: *and platted a crown of thorns and put it about his head*.

8　**forgiveness** see St Luke's account of the crucifixion: *Jesus said, Father, forgive them; for they know not what they do (St Luke 23: 34)*.

9-14　How successful is the sestet? Does the gulf between the intense religious thinking of lines 1–8 and the (boastful?) recollections of *my profane mistresses* (10) point to the deeply divided state of the poet's soul, or is the whole poem trivialized by the comparison between divine and earthly love?

14　**This beauteous form** the difficulty here is that the poem depends upon the link, in both mistresses and Christ, between beauty and pity. Is Christ presented in lines 1–8 as beautiful? You might feel there is beauty in the care with which the poet imagines Christ or that the details are ugly and repulsive.

Holy sonnet 14

Nowhere else in Donne's religious poetry is the drama and the contradictory violence of paradox so evident as in this sonnet. There is something thrilling, even exhilarating, about the lightness and speed with which the poet moves from one to another and the way the paradoxes mount to the breathtaking (and outrageous?) climax of the closing couplet. Yet the paradoxes are questionable as well as exciting: readers may wish to ask whether they are attempts to renew a jaded religious language, or whether the poet has become so fascinated with playing games with words that the poem merely delights in contradictions.

1   **my . . . you** as in many of the love poems an examination of the frequency and impact of the first and second person pronouns is illuminating.

2,4   The fourth line 'answers' the second by providing stronger verbs: for instance, *break* in place of *knock*. Should these juxtapositions be read as appropriate because of the desperate state of the poet, or does the fourth line disturb because of its almost blasphemous substitution of violent words for ones which are steeped in biblical associations? Christ in *Revelation* 3: 20 is imagined as saying: *Behold I stand at the door and knock*, whereas in *St. Matthew* 6: 19 it is thieves who *break through and steal.*

5   **usurped town** a town in which power has illegally (and probably violently) passed from a legitimate ruler to an invader.

5   **another** it is not clear who or what *another* is; it could be the devil, death, sin, doubt, despair or a human lover.

7   **viceroy** one who wields power on behalf of a supreme (and usually absent) ruler.

9   **fain** willingly or gladly. See Approaches p. 133.

11   **Divorce** are both this word and the rest of the line effective or repellent? It can be read as an essential word in an implied story which acts as a parallel to the poet's religious state: a woman has desperately fallen in love (9) but is betrothed, married or has been stolen by another so cannot be *free* (13) or *chaste* (14) (the word was applied to married couples) until her true love divorces her from the one to whom she is bound. But since such an idea is hardly

Christian (the Anglican marriage service insists *Those whom God hath joined together let no man put asunder*) it might be read as the poet indulging a love of paradox at the expense of the word's meaning. In short: could the word *divorce* ever be appropriately used of God's relationships with his people?

Holy sonnet 17

An autobiographical approach is difficult to avoid here: the poet's wife, Ann Donne, died on 15 August 1617, seven days after giving birth to their twelfth child. She was 33. The poem might not have been written immediately afterwards; Helen Gardner thinks that it might date from 1619. It is a poem of strong feelings, which the poet hardly seems to understand fully. Consequently, it is not easy to decide whether it is essentially about human or divine love. A further problem is that it seems unfinished; given the attitude of God to the poet (9-14), the reader looks for the poet's response but finds none. It may be that what is fascinating (and moving?) about the sonnet is the poet's uncertainty about the nature and the rightness of his desires and his less than successful attempt to accept the situation in which he has found himself.

1-4   Some critics have said that the poem is concerned with the poet's grief. Is this the case? The logical *Since*, the conventional characterization of death as paying a *debt/To nature* and the possible reading of the second line to mean that her death is for her and his good all suggest that the poet accepts his loss with little or no anguish. The argument for there being grief rests on a consideration of the sonnet's rhythms: do the heavy stresses at the end of the first line, the way the rhythm singles out the painful word early and the manner in which the sense of the sentence leads up to *Wholly* indicate that the words issue from a deeply-felt grief?

3   **ravished** this can mean being sexually possessed as well as carried away.

4   **Wholly** is there a pun on holy?

5   **whet** sharpen and make ready.

6   **seek thee God** to what extent is this a poem of human or divine

love? The cadence leading up to God makes it one of the strongest climaxes in the poem, yet readers should observe the change the sentence undergoes with the introduction of *But* (7).

8   **a holy thirsty dropsy melts me** is his desire religious, sexual or a fusion of both? The first adjective is *holy*, and *thirsty* can apply to both divine and human love, but *melts* (emotionally affects) is more appropriate to love poetry.

9-10   Which picture of love is the controlling image of these two lines? Is God offering his love to the poet *instead* of that of the dead beloved, or is God cast in the role of a father who supplies a handsome dowry (*offering all thine*) in exchange for the heavenly marriage of the poet and his dead beloved?

13   **tender** how does this adjective function? Does it show that the poet recognizes that, in spite of his pain, God is compassionate, or does it so clash with *jealousy* as to show the poet's ambivalent feelings about what God has done to him - that is, taken away his beloved?

13   **doubt** fear and suspect.

Holy sonnet 19

This sonnet is different from many of the others in that there is no attempt to imagine the Last Judgement or the figure of Death or the crucified Christ; instead, the poet is entirely preoccupied with the puzzling and morally distressing changes in his own spiritual state. Two problems are raised by this: the first is whether the narrowness of subject matter makes the sonnet more or less impressive than the others; the second is whether the concern for the self and the concern for the poem as a poem (*contraries* meeting in *one* is a good description of the tensions of the poem itself) run counter to the religious anguish of a man who is appalled at his own spiritual instability. In the light of the above, a performance of the poem would have to be very sensitive to the rapid changes of tone, pace and cadence.

1   **vex** the word had a much stronger meaning in the seventeenth century than it has today, being closer to shaken with anguish.

2-3   **Inconstancy/constant** does the verbal play upon this paradox heighten or diminish the sense of the poet's distress?

4   **vows** the relationship between religious poetry and love poetry which emerges in some of the Holy Sonnets is present in this and other words in the poem.

5   **humorous** changeable.

5   **contrition** being sorry for one's sins.

7   **riddlingly distempered** his contrition wildly swings from one extreme to another as if he were unbalanced by disease.

9   **I durst** unlike some of the other sonnets there is not a sharp break between the octave and the sestet. Does this make it an impressively concentrated poem, or does the reader miss the drama of a change from one mood to another?

11   **rod** God's justice and punishment are frequently spoken of as a rod.

13   **fantastic** uncertain, extreme, unpredictable.

13   **ague** a disease or fever.

13-14   Does the paradox of his *best days* (a phrase often used when talking about health) being those when he *shake(s) with fear* successfully sum up the contraries of the poem, or is it just an example of the poet's love of verbal play?

Good Friday, 1613. Riding Westward

This poem opens in a vein of intellectual speculation and closes with ardent begging that God will redeem him. The two elements provide a clue to its character: the poet is self-consciously aware that his physical situation accurately mirrors the state of his relationship to God, and thus there is a blend of pleasure in achieving such an appropriate poetic image with real anguish at his spiritual state. In keeping with the poetic, that is to say the constructed or fabricated, manner of the poem, what is seen is the product not of the physical eye but of the imagination. In line 33 he says that the Cross of Christ is far *from mine eye*, and in line 35 there is a telling picture of the guilty poet with his back to Christ yet his memory fixed on him. See Approaches p. 141.

1-10   Medieval astronomy claimed that each planet consisted of a *sphere* controlled by an *intelligence* or spirit. However, a planet could come under the influence of another more powerful agent and so be governed by it rather than following its natural course – (*natural form*) (6). In the case of spheres the natural direction was thought to be from west to east, but so powerful was the Primum Mobile (in Donne's analogy the *first mover* (8)) that they actually travelled in the reverse direction.

8   **whirled** there might be a pun here.

11   **sun** another pun?

11   **rising** *rising* could mean the incarnation of Christ, the physical lifting up of the cross or the resurrection.

13   **But that** except that.

17   This is a common biblical idea: *Thou canst not see my face: for there shall no man see me and live* (*Exodus* 33: 20).

19-20   The *New Testament* says that the crucifixion of Jesus was accompanied by darkness - *darkness over all the land* (*St Matthew* 27: 45), and that at his death there was an earthquake - *and the earth did shake, and the stones were cloven* (*St Matthew* 27: 51). The word *lieutenant* is Donne's own metaphor for nature as God's second in command; *footstool* is a biblical metaphor for the earth being under God's authority - *the earth is my footstool* (*Isaiah* 66: 1).

24   **Zenith . . . antipodes** wherever one is on earth (*antipodes* means its furthest points) God is an absolute distance from us.

25-6   Some believed that souls had their seat or basis in blood, but theologians questioned whether this could apply to Christ (*if not of his*). There was agreement, however, that since salvation came through the cross, all souls rested in Christ's blood.

29-32   A traditional element of Christian devotion was a contemplation of the figure of Mary, the Mother of Jesus, particularly in her presence at the crucifixion. Mary was God's partner because she agreed to bear the Christ child and thus she provided *Half of that sacrifice* by which the world was redeemed (*ransomed*).

36   **tree** the cross.

37   **but** only.

38   **Corrections** punishments aimed at reforming him.

38   **leave** stop.

39-40   Compare the violence of these pleas (demands?) with the language of *Holy sonnet 14* (1-4). How strong in both is the idea that the poet would rather be the object of God's anger than be ignored?

41   **Restore thine image** salvation was thought of as a return to

mankind's original estate, when the image of God was clearly present in people.

A Hymn to Christ, at the Author's last going into Germany

This poem has a grave, meditative tone; the poet seriously spells out to himself (this process can be heard in the strong monosyllabic thrust of many of the words) the situation he finds himself in, and through a consideration of weighty issues - death, providence, the nature of love - he moves towards a climactic decision. A problem the reader may have is that of following the poem's reasoning: you may ask yourself whether there are too many ideas present and whether the argument moves too quickly. Another problem is that the poem is the product of a profound religious faith, which modern readers might find difficult to appreciate.

Title On 12 May 1619 Donne sailed as chaplain with the Earl of Doncaster's diplomatic mission to the German Princes. Shortly before he left he preached a farewell sermon at Lincoln's Inn in which he spoke of the sea as *the Sea of his blood*.

2 **my emblem of thy ark** an emblem was an image which represented a quality or idea in a system of thought; it was usually used as a teaching device and was often accompanied by a woodcut and a short poem giving a moral comment. Here the poet makes a traditional association between a ship and Noah's ark, which survived the Flood. The ark is emblematic of Divine providence and the Church.

4 **blood** the word *blood* stands for the redemption of mankind by the cross of Christ.

8 **never** consider the emphatic stress upon this word. Is it a stress of unswerving conviction, or is there an element of bravado in it, possibly arising from doubt or fear?

9 **sacrifice** the word *sacrifice* includes the idea that he renounces his earthly and temporal loves and that he gives them, or offers them, to God.

9 **Island** England.

12 **thy sea** see note on line 4.

14 **winter** the word not only suggests age but also the loss of earthly pleasure and the absence of his own inner, or spiritual, resources. It is, however, interesting to note that in a line that effectively says he is nothing, there is one of Donne's characteristic poetic flourishes – a repeated word which yet has significantly different meanings.

17 **control** in a soul which is whole and integrated (*harmonious*) there is no need for Christ or the Church to check or restrain (*control*) its love.

18 **amorousness** this word might seem to be more suggestive of earthly and even erotic love than the love the soul has for God: does it indicate the struggle the poet has in renouncing earthly ties or does it try to show that the passions and longings of carnal love are actually akin to divine love and that the word is therefore appropriate? (This question can be asked of some of the other religious poems.)

20 **jealous** the idea that God possessively loves and guards all that belongs to him frequently occurs in *The Bible: for I am the Lord, thy God, a jealous God* (*Exodus* 20:5). Here Christ is the jealous lover.

21-2 See *Holy sonnet 17* (9-10).

22 **who ever gives, takes liberty** this could either mean that giving one's love is not always justified (that is, one takes a liberty in doing so), or whoever gives someone love takes away that person's freedom.

25 **divorce** see note on *Holy sonnet 14* (11).

26 **fainter beams** the beams of the sun are often symbols of God's or Christ's (there is a pun on son) love for the world.

28 **hopes** worldly prospects such as a place in the life of the court.

29 Consider the place in this and other religious poems of how negation - lack of light, lack of love, lack of success - is the way to God. To what extent in Donne is it the absence of things (even the absence of religious experience) that brings the poet to God?

30 **I go out of sight** is this best read as 'I travel far away' or 'I die'?

32 What kind of conclusion is this? Does the dark and long falling cadence close the poem heavily and gloomily, or is there a distinctive triumph in that the poet has freely chosen *night* rather than worldly pleasures (28) knowing it will bring him to God?

Hymn to God my God, in my Sickness

Perhaps the most remarkable aspect of this poem is its serene tone. There is no apparent anguish, and, unlike some of the Holy Sonnets, the many paradoxes and polarities (for instance: *do/think* (5), *west/east* (13), *death/resurrection* (15)) are not born out of spiritual turmoil, and, what is more, they are neatly resolved. Such neatness makes the poem intellectually elegant; to use a metaphor from the poem itself, everything is mapped out with a satisfying clarity. Even the potential violence of the last line could be allayed by seeing that the idea is not a sudden dramatic outburst but a *text* carefully chosen by the preacher in which *throws down* is balanced by the religiously important word *raise*. Still, some readers might be troubled by the poem's contemplative calm: is it too assured and are its paradoxes too slick? A reply might be that its success lies in capturing the experience that is said to occur to many sick or dying people of feeling happily released from the body's pain and free to view oneself in a detached and spiritually calm way.

Title   Isaac Walton claimed that the poem was written during Donne's final illness in 1631, but it may have been composed during or shortly after a serious illness he suffered in 1623.

1   **holy room** heaven.

4   **I tune the instrument** a musician, being only an employee, would tune his instrument before entering the banqueting hall of a mansion. Does the image work better if it is interpreted as meaning prepare oneself with prayers before death or practise the art of poetry so that the harmony of verse may anticipate the harmony of the *choir of saints* (2)?

5   **before** this word draws attention to how the opening stanza is separated from the others: how should the relation between it and the rest of the poem be understood? Does the musical imagery successfully prepare us for the emotionally composed and serene tone of the poem, or is the jump from a domestic setting to the furthest parts of the world so extreme as to cut this stanza off damagingly from the rest?

6   **love** the doctors' loving concern for him.

7   **Cosmographers . . . map** because, according to a common contem-

porary idea, a person was a little world, it is poetically appropriate to see his *physicians* as geographers (*cosmographers*) examining a map of the world.

9 **my south-west discovery** one of the preoccupations of seamanship was the locating of passages or routes (called discoveries) into distant parts of the world. Here the geographical image functions figuratively: south is the region of heat and west is where the sun sets; that is to say, he expects to die as the result of a fever.

10 *Per fretum febris* this means both 'through the raging fever' and 'through the strait of fever'.

10 **straits** this can mean a narrow passage of sea water, the trials and difficulties of life and the hard way to salvation.

11 **I joy** is the poet fully aware of his plight and yet able to rejoice at the prospect of death, or is he only confident (over-confident?) because he has avoided the reality of death by, so to speak, disguising it in elegant and intellectually clever imagery?

13-14 Donne makes this point in one of his sermons: *but to paste that flat Map upon a round body, and then West and East are all one.* In theological terms *west* is death and *east* symbolizes the resurrection.

16-17 Behind these images there lies the once much-debated question of where the earthly paradise of Eden was. As candidates for the earthly paradise they all function figuratively as images of heaven: *Pacific* means peaceful; *Jerusalem* as well as being an image of heaven means vision of peace, and *eastern riches* is reminiscent of the imagery in the *Gospels* for the Kingdom of Heaven – treasure and great pearls.

18 The *Anyan* straits were supposed to separate North America from Asia. The straits of *Magellan* are at the foot of South America, and the Mediterranean sea is entered through the straits of *Gibraltar*.

20 It was traditionally believed that after the biblical flood the world was divided between the sons of Noah: Japheth (*Japhet*) was given Europe, Ham (*Cham*) Africa and *Shem* Asia.

21-2 Having wondered, according to the conceit of his body as a map, where paradise is located (16-17), he now settles on the belief, most prevalent at the time, that since Eden was located in Mesopotamia it was in the same region (*stood in one place*) as Jerusalem, where Christ was crucified. There are also legends about how the wood for Christ's cross came from a tree that grew out of the bones of Adam.

St. Paul frequently compares Adam to Christ; for instance: *For as in Adam all die, even so in Christ shall all be made alive* (I Corinthians 15: 22). Christ is also *the last Adam* (I Corinthians 15: 45).

24 **sweat** because Adam brought death into the world through the fall, the feverish sweat which covers the poet is that of *the first Adam*.

25 **blood** see note on *A Hymn to Christ, at the Author's last going into Germany* (4).

26 **purple** the conceit is that Christ's blood is like a robe of royal purple.

27 **thorns . . . other crown** *thorns* could mean the crown of thorns which Christ wore when he bought salvation on the cross, or the poet could figuratively be referring to his own sufferings as being like a crown of thorns. The *other crown* is the heavenly crown worn by those in heaven.

29 **to mine own** to myself.

30 Strictly speaking this is not a biblical text. Nevertheless, it reflects biblical thinking in its paradox that those who are raised are those that have been thrown down.

A Hymn to God the Father

Walton records that this poem was written during Donne's illness of 1623. Its tone, imagery, argument and manner may, therefore, be usefully compared to *Hymn to God my God, in my Sickness*, which may have been written at the same time. The movement and tone are memorable: its pace is measured, and in the gravity and honesty of its brooding self-questioning there is a dark yet dignified progress towards the final plea and the undemonstrative assurance of the close. The big problem of the poem is whether that tone is consistently maintained: is this a poem in which the mind of the poet is concentrated with moving seriousness upon his relationship with God, or is he, at points, preoccupied with his own skill as a poet in exploiting the possibilities of language?

Title Why is the poem addressed to *God the Father*? In the closing stanza there is a pun on Christ as the Son of God and the *sun*: should the poem be read as being about the salvation brought by the Son of

God, or should it be interpreted as the humble request of a man who wants God the Father to accept him as a son? Can it be both?

1-12 There are four questions in the first two stanzas; if you try reading them aloud you may notice that, unusually, the final cadence falls rather than rises. What is the effect of this? Does it suggest that the poet is assured of salvation so the question is not a real one or, conversely, that he is so absorbed in meditating upon his unworthiness that he dare not question God in an ordinary way?

1 **begun** according to Christian doctrine all of humanity are marked by the fall of Adam (*Genesis* 3) and thus bear his guilt. This is called original sin. It was sometimes thought of as being transmitted from one generation to another through procreation. Hence when he *begun* he was a sinner.

5 **done** should a man who is so aware of his need for God's mercy allow himself the poetic indulgence of a pun on his own name. Either the introduction of the pun is a flaw because it detracts from the weighty seriousness of the poem's tone, or it is a daring and successful way of showing how delightful it would be to be possessed and owned by God. See Approaches p. 133.

6 **more** some critics see a pun here on Donne's wife's name – Ann More.

7 **that sin** the sin could be any wrong deed that led others astray, or, more specifically, the writing of sexually-arousing poetry.

10 **wallowed** this could be a comic moment of self-mockery where he pictures himself grotesquely indulging in sin. Another possibility is that given the strong traditional association between *wallowing* and pigs, the poet is imagining himself in the role of the prodigal son (*St Luke* 15: 11-32) who, in his poverty, was forced to mind pigs before he came to his senses and returned to his father.

13 **fear** the fear is that he might not be saved. To despair of the possibility of one's own salvation was thought to be the worst spiritual state into which one could fall.

14 **thread** life was sometimes pictured as a thread spun out and finally cut by the fates; here, however, the poet spins his own life and is, consequently, solely responsible for all his wrongdoing.

14 **perish** it is perhaps significant that in the Authorized Version of *The Bible* this word appears in the story of the prodigal son: *and I perish with hunger! I will arise and go to my father* (*St Luke* 15: 17-18). See Approaches p. 152.

14 **shore** which way does this image work? Is he the drowning ship-

wrecked sailor who dies just as he reaches the shore, or is the sea a symbol of God which the poet fails to attain because he dies on the shore?

16 **heretofore** Donne may be thinking of the words of Jesus: *he God maketh his sun to rise on the evil and on the good* (St Matthew 5: 45).

17 **thou hast done** if the pun works, this is its triumphant resolution: the work of Christ is completed and Donne's salvation is secured because God takes him as his own.

Approaches

Appendices

Donne and love

In Donne's love poetry there is a marked diversity of moods and attitudes: some poems are purely physical in that the poet only appears to be interested in the woman's body, while others celebrate a love so refined that it is inner beauty alone that attracts him. In some poems constancy is praised, while in others there is a casual acceptance of both female and male unfaithfulness, and some poems see love as above time while others are about partings and affairs that have come to an end.

As with any body of literature that is richly varied, we look for the outlines of groupings. Two suggest themselves: there are poems on the joys of love and poems on its trials and sorrows.

In some poems there are the joys of discovering a beloved, the pleasures of sharing feelings and the wonder that lovers remain faithful to each other. Other poems, however, deal with the anguish of unreturned love, the bitterness of rejection and the selfish pleasures of a man who is out to conquer.

Which do you think are dominant? Is Donne mainly (or most successfully) a poet of the heights of love – its joys and ecstasies – or is he more concerned with (and better at presenting) its miseries, failures, resentments and destructive passions? But as you think through that question (and you may find that each time you read Donne you come up with a different answer) you may decide that such a two-fold grouping of poems is far too simple. It is helpful, therefore, to look in more detail at some of the kinds of poems included in this selection.

Different kinds of love poems

There are poems - *The Anniversary, The Canonization, The Good Morrow, The Sun Rising* - that celebrate the union in love of body and soul. These present lovers as kings and saints, whose love is so far above that of ordinary mortals that it never decays or dies. These poems are physically and intellectually exuberant. In two poems - *The Relic, The Undertaking* - the love is joyful but platonic in character; that is to say, it is the soul and not the body which is the object of love. Yet another way of celebrating the joys of love is to give rein to far-ranging thought. In *The Ecstasy, Lover's Infiniteness* and *Love's Growth* the wonder of love (never absent from the poems mentioned above) prompts complex and subtle speculation about the nature of love itself.

There are poems on the trials of love which present the male lover as an unsuccessful suitor. In *The Funeral* and *Twicknam Garden* the poet loves a girl who does not love him. In *A Jet Ring Sent* and, probably, *The Triple Fool* the lover has actually been rejected. In two poems, however, the position is reversed: *The Apparition* and *Woman's Constancy* show the poet relishing, even gloating over, the power he has over a woman. Male power of one kind or another is a prominent feature of a number of poems. The lover in *Elegy 4* is smugly pleased with his success in loving and frustrated by those who want to make his life difficult. *The Damp, The Dream, The Flea* and *Elegy 19* might be said to be wooing, or, to put the point more bluntly, seduction poems in that they use a number of emotional and intellectual ploys to make the woman comply with the man's desires. Male power is implied in *Song: Go, and catch a falling star*, but it is the power of the cynic over the lover. One poem seems wholly cynical – *Love's Alchemy*. It is best understood as a palinode – a poem which reverses or rejects what was said in an earlier poem. It can, thus, be read as a reversal of *The Relic* or *The Undertaking* in its cynical dismissal of platonic love.

There are a group of poems about parting. *The Expiration, Song: Sweetest love, A Valediction: forbidding Mourning, Elegy 5* and *Elegy 16*. It is not clear whether these should be thought of as poems on the joys or the trials of love. The tone of *A Valediction: forbidding Mourning* is very close to the platonic love poems, and in *Song: Sweetest love* the quality of love is very similar to *The Good Morrow*. There is, nevertheless, real pain;

think, for instance, about the dangers outlined in *Elegy 16*. The two poems on death or the nearness of death – *The Fever*, *A Nocturnal upon S. Lucy's Day, being the shortest day* – are problematic in the same way: the love is deep, and the pain is very real.

To group poems in this way is to draw a kind of 'map' of the territory of Donne's verse: although a 'map' cannot indicate how subtly varied the ground is, it can help newcomers to find their way about and can show them where the difficult areas are. These difficult areas are the issues raised by the verse. One – male power – is mentioned above, there are several others, and they are all very teasing.

The emphasis on the physical

Some of the poems deal with the sexual character of the relationships between men and women; they are not just concerned with desire and longing but with physical consummation. But this presents a problem: are some of the poems so preoccupied with the physical that love comes to mean no more than sexual intercourse?

Take the example of *The Dream*. At one point the poet delights in the wonderful fact that the beloved is who she is:

> I must confess, it could not choose but be
> Profane, to think thee anything but thee.
>
> (19-20)

But later the tone changes; no longer is there the breathless religious awe which dismisses comparative language as Profane but an unoriginal play upon the lighting of torches and sexual arousal:

> Perchance as torches which must ready be,
> Men light and put out, so thou deal'st with me
>
> (27-28)

Can a reader resist the conclusion that the awe and wonder felt in the presence of the beloved's unique nature has been reduced to the hope that his sexual desires (the touch is a conventional phallic symbol) will be fulfilled?

But if this is so, there is something strange about Donne's sexual language. The issue can be put in this way: does Donne's language actually express the physical pleasures of love? In *Elegy 19* (a poem which C.S. Lewis said was *Intended to arouse the appetite it describes*) there are these boldly intimate lines:

> License my roving hands, and let them go
> Before, behind, between, above, below.
>
> (25-6)

It is important to ask what these words appeal to: is it to the senses or the mind? The prepositional intimacy – *Before, behind, between ...* – enjoyed by the *roving hands* might stimulate the senses of a reader (though perhaps only a male one?) but equally a reader may decide that the language does not disclose what the woman's body feels like and that, consequently, the reader *knows* what the poet is feeling without *sharing* the same sensations. It is worth asking this question about the poems that deal frankly with sexual love.

Male dominance

The issue of male dominance can be raised by looking at how *Elegy 19* develops. The poem continues with a geographical conceit (see Approaches p. 158) *my America, my new found land,* the poet cries as he feels the body of his mistress. The joy at possessing a beautiful body may be one which can be shared by both men and women. But what is to be made of the way the poet extends the conceit? He calls her *My mine of precious stones, my empery*. That can be read as the language of economic exploitation and political dominance: she is like a mine full of precious stones and she is also a colony in his empire.

Poetry such as this sharply raises the issue of whether Donne's poetry is too readily at home with the image of the self-seeking male, who enjoys exercising power over women. This question may be asked from the perspective of the reader: can a female reader warmly respond to the images of masterful male dominance and female passivity?

Significantly different ways to the poem?

Many people have recently become aware that relationships between men and women have often been conducted on some shared yet unquestioned assumptions about sexual roles. Men have been thought of as actively seeking sexual pleasure, and women have, consequently, been understood as objects upon which men can gratify themselves.

Elegy 19 may be an extreme case, but those who have reservations about Donne's poetry because it habitually takes this stance can find other evidence. The first two stanzas of *The Canonization* are about his love rather than hers; the attitude to women at the close of *Love's Alchemy* is so contemptuous that some readers may find it grossly offensive, and the roles in *Elegy 16* are such as to make the man's life attractive and adventurous and the woman's domestic and ordinary.

But, as in most of the problems with Donne there is another side to the argument.

Three things can be said. The first is that in Donne's day, it was accepted that the man was active in love and the woman passive. The second is that in both the poems on the joys of love and those on its trials women are sometimes presented very positively. The mutual love – the equal giving and receiving of love – of *The Good Morrow* and *A Valediction: forbidding Mourning* implicitly elevates the importance of women, and in *The Sun Rising* the praise the poet gives to his beloved is lavish yet not such as to diminish her into a passive and pretty plaything. The third thing is that Donne might be showing that love is often a struggle rather than a harmonious relationship and that a battle for power is as common in love as the mutual sharing of feeling and interests.

Egotism in the love poetry

The issue of male power is an aspect of one of the most difficult things about Donne's poetry – egotism. There is in poem after poem an unabashed concentration upon the self. This takes several forms. In *Love's Growth* there is amazement at the quality of the speaker's own experience:

> I scarce believe my love to be so pure. (1)

In *Love's Alchemy* the self's relentless pursuit of pleasure, includes talking about personal conquests in love:

> I have loved, and got, and told. (3)

and in *The Canonization* the speaker parades his sensitivity before his audience in the following example:

> Alas, alas, who's injured by my love? (10)

The speakers in the poems often seek gratification through emotional and intellectual power. Emotional power is evident in the way a poet often presents himself as free from the inhibiting fears that prevent women from submitting to him, and intellectual power is exerted through the patient (and possibly patronizing) step-by-step arguments and dazzling flashes of verbal ingenuity. Both these qualities can be seen in *The Flea*: the poet presents himself as having advanced beyond the fears of his mistress, and the entire poem can be seen as an argument (a deliberately outrageous one?) which leads to the inevitable conclusion that she should yield to him. Another poem which displays the egotistical use of emotional and intellectual power is *Woman's Constancy*. The emotional power is present in the trick of pretending to be under her power when, as the close reveals, he is not, and the intellectual power is present in the way in which her arguments for leaving him are, in actual fact, ones which he has invented. In lines 14-15 he says that in the face of the arguments that she supposedly supplies he *could/Dispute, and conquer*. They are revealing words: the powers of the mind can be used not just to enter into debate, not just to win an argument but actually to conquer another.

There is another aspect to egotism. One of the difficult things about Donne's poetry is the tension between the poet's concern for his beloved and a fascination with new ideas and the complexity of his own mental processes.

Activity

Read the opening of *A Valediction: forbidding Mourning* and ask yourself to what extent the poet is concerned with his feelings for his beloved and to what extent with the processes of his own thought:

As virtuous men pass mildly away,
    And whisper to their souls, to go,
Whilst some of their sad friends do say,
    The breath goes now, and some say, no:

So let us melt, and make no noise,
    No tear-floods, nor sigh-tempests move,
'Twere profanation of our joys
    To tell the laity our love.

(1-8)

Discussion

The fact that the poem begins with a lengthy analogy about how *virtuous* men die, which is then applied to the lovers - *So let us melt* - might suggest that it is ideas that are uppermost in the poet's mind. Such a view is strengthened by the way the poet evidently enjoys coneying the uncertainty of the friends - *The breath goes now, and some say, no* - and the tilt he takes at the conventional image of lovers who weep floods of tears and sigh mighty winds - *No tear-floods, nor sigh-tempests move.* In short, the verses can be read as the work of a man who likes ideas. But they can also be read another way. Note, for instance, the ease with which he moves from the image of the dying man to their own predicament. The sounds of the words act out a strangely touching blend of harmony and pain: harmony because *no* at the end of the first verse rhymes with *So* at the beginning of the second, and pain because the 'o' sound (also present in *goes*, and the *no* in the fifth line) is traditionally the poetic sound of regret, grief and unfulfilled longing. Note also that there are no singulars: the poet says *let us melt,* and goes on to speak of profaning *our joys* if the laity were told of *our love.* If both readings are possible, how can the two verses be described? Should we speak of a tension between egotism and loving concern or about egotism subdued or even overcome by loving attention? It is perhaps even more important to ask whether this, and other poems, are emotionally stable. It may be that one of the exciting things about reading Donne is never being certain whether love will dwindle into egotism or egotism give way to love.

The poetry of love and passion?

That last sentence touches upon the most difficult question of all. Given that the poetry might sometimes stress the physical at the expense of other aspects of sexuality, and given that the poet often adopts aggressively male attitudes, and displays, at times, an egotistical posture, should we call this body of verse *love* poetry at all? The word *love* is commonly used in a number of ways, but if it is to be used without distortion there must be something present other than longing or desire. That *something* must be a recognition and concern for what another person is thinking and feeling. Is this the case in Donne? Little time need be spent on *Love's Alchemy:* it is a love poem only in the negative sense of explicitly denying what most lovers claim. A more interesting, and certainly more difficult, case is *A Fever:* it opens with what appears to be real anguish, but when in the fourth verse he debates the end of the world, is anguish (and therefore love) present? In *The Undertaking* the poet is proud of what he has done – loving the inner loveliness of a woman – but what evidence is there that they share feelings or that he is concerned or knows about what she is undergoing? Such an interpretation suggests that instead of talking about Donne's love poetry we should call it, or some of the poems at least, poetry of desire, passion or longing.

However, you may wish to insist that some poems are clearly about love in the usual sense of that word. *The Anniversary*, *The Good Morrow*, *A Nocturnal upon S. Lucy's Day*, *being the shortest day* and *The Sun Rising* all show a true regard for the beloved, and the unity of the lovers is the central point of *The Ecstasy*. It is, however, worth asking whether it is quite as simple as that. In *The Good Morrow* a *thou* and an *I* unite in the first two lines to become a *we*. Is this grammatical transformation not an expression of their mutual love? You may think that this is all that needs to be said. On the other hand, who is it that feels the love to be mutual? The poet certainly does: but what evidence is there that he recognizes that she does as well? The question can be asked of other poems. On occasions you may feel he is only concerned with what he thinks and feels, and on others you might be aware of the loving attention he pays to his beloved. His poetry is as teasingly enigmatic as that.

Is the 'I' of the poems John Donne?

So far, we have assumed that the speaker in the poems is usually John Donne. The language is certainly Donne's. However, this does not mean that whenever the word *I* appears that *I* is the man John Donne. This is an important issue: should we read the poems confessionally, that is, as expressions of what John Donne thought, or should we read them fictively, that is, as works of imagination in which the *I* is fashioned for the purposes of the poem and the incidents presented have no relationship to Donne's own life? In the Notes the modern convention of calling the *I* of the poem *the poet* has been adopted except where matters of language and poetic structure are concerned, when *Donne* is used. This convention prevents a reader from simply adopting a confessional interpretation. I

127

have done this because it is important to remember that art is not a direct transcription from life.

Nevertheless, in the case of Donne nothing is simple. The religious poems, for instance, probably display a much stronger link with Donne's life than some of the love poems. The Holy Sonnets come from that period of life when he was moving, though possibly unawares, from the hope of a secular post to the decision to become a clergyman. This is not to say that the religious poems are autobiographical but to suggest that they are imaginative recreations of his own experiences. This point can be extended. If the love poems are entirely fictive this does not rule out the possibility that they bear the stamp of Donne in their emotional force and intellectual attitudes. A further question is that of consistency. If, in spite of the variety, you feel there is a similar attitude to experience you might be inclined to see them as expressions of what John Donne felt and thought. You should, however, remember that completely fictional works can be consistent.

Donne and religion

Writing religious verse

It is very easy to fall into the error of assuming that when Donne was young, vigorous and adventurous he wrote love poems but that when he grew older, feebler and more conventional he turned to religion and wrote religious (or divine) poetry. This view fails to do justice to the overwhelming importance of religion in Donne's day, nor does it fit in with what we know of Donne's life. Donne became a clergyman in 1615, at the age of 43. It is clear, however, that he was writing religious verse before that date. One poem's title is *Good Friday, 1613. Riding Westward* (there is no reason to suppose it is fictional) and the weight of critical opinion suggests that many of the Holy Sonnets were written as early as 1609. Moreover, Donne's first biographer, Isaac Walton, presents him as a man who was concerned with religious questions in his youth as well as in his maturity. This is not to deny that many of his love poems were written when he was younger, but it is to insist that Donne was concerned with religious questions for most of his life.

It is, then, not surprising that there are continuities between the love and the religious poems. The love poems employ religious language. *The Canonization* and *The Relic,* for instance, are based upon a sustained application of religious ideas to lovers. In some love poems the tone and the verbal music – the sounds and rhythms of the words – have a religious quality.

Given the continuities of language and movement a way into the religious verse is to see how some of the characteristics of the love poetry are present in the divine poems. We shall examine three features in this light, and a further three distinctive features of his religious poetry.

The power of argument

In the love poetry arguments abound. Is there a similar interest in the religious poems? Intellectual issues are certainly present: think about the geographical, as well as the theological, debates in *Hymn to God my God, in my Sickness* or the academic learning that is present in *Good Friday, 1613. Riding Westward.*

What *purpose* does argument serve in the divine poems? It is useful to compare the religious poems with the love poetry. In the love poems the poet explores ideas and seeks to explain them, but, above all, he uses argument to *persuade.* The love poetry is charged with *masculine persuasive force (Elegy 16* (4)). Does this apply to the divine poems? On the level of grammar this appears to be the case; the grammatical mood of *Holy sonnets 6, 7, 14* is, to use a technical term, imperative - the poet uses argument to tell, even *order,* God to act. But two things should be noticed: the first is that it is God to whom the poet speaks. A mistress might be persuaded or forced to act against her will, but not God. The second is that what the poet demands has already been done by God – securing the means of salvation. *Holy sonnet 7* ends with the poet saying, still in imperatives, that God should teach him *how to repent*, adding, almost as an after thought, that *that's as good/As if thou had'st sealed my pardon, with thy blood.* The *As if* cannot be read straightforwardly or innocently, because in Christian theology there can be no doubt that through the cross of Christ God has already sealed the pardon of the world. It is not easy to characterize the effect this has upon argument, nor is it easy to be clear about its significance. You may, however, wish to think about two things: the first is that the fact that the poet argues with the one with whom no argument is possible might make him seem small, foolish, pathetic or even absurd. The second thing to consider is whether the heat of the argument, particularly when it is about what God has already done, has the effect of making God powerful and mighty. In short, it could be that although the effort of the argument comes from man, its effect is to make God look strong.

Egotism in the religious poetry

One way of seeing how concerned the poet is with himself is to count the number of personal pronouns in a poem. In *Holy sonnet 6* my occurs ten times, and *I* and *me* twice. There are fewer personal pronouns in number 7, but it could be argued that their impact is great because they all appear in the sestet. Another indicator of egotism, or, at least, a preoccupation with the concrete nature of individual experience, may be found in language which forcefully specifies time and place.

Activity

Think about the effect of *this, here* and *these* in the context of the poems in which they occur.

This is my play's last scene	(*Holy sonnet 6* (1))
here on this lowly ground	(*Holy sonnet 7* (12))

save that here
These are my best days   (*Holy sonnet 19* (13–14))
  as I come
I tune my instrument here at the door
                                          (*Hymn to God, my God,
                                          in my Sickness* (3–4))

Discussion

The words are not directly used of the self, but their presence helps to
make the self more vivid because they direct the reader to the fact that
human experience is always rooted in one place and happens in one
instant of time.

The egotism of the love poems might be felt to be disturbing.
Egotism in religious poetry is even more problematic. Just how
difficult the issue of religious poetry is may be seen by thinking
about a famous remark that the eighteenth-century scholar and
poet, Dr Johnson, made about religious, or devotional poetry.
His argument was that the communion between *God and the
human soul* is so elevated that it *cannot be poetical.* He added that
a man imploring the mercy of God *is already in a higher state than
poetry can confer.* (The last remark is of particular relevance to
Donne, because, as will be stressed later, pleading for mercy is
one of his central concerns.) The thrust of Johnson's words is
that someone in prayer is already beyond the need for poetic
expression, so that verse is religiously irrelevant and poetically
inadequate.

At least two responses are possible to the problem that Dr
Johnson has focused upon. One is to take the line of argument
that was explored in the first section of Approaches and ask
whether these poems actually are religious. It could be that
though they use religious language their real nature is non-
religious in that they are concerned not with a relationship
with God but with the state of the human mind. One poem,
Holy sonnet 19, is not about God at all but is preoccupied with
the divided state of the poet's soul. It is a short step from that
to seeing all the poems as being concerned with the poet's own

self. The other option is to claim that they are rightly called religious poems and that the prominence of the self, in spite of Johnson, is an important element in characterizing their particular quality. The crucial question to ask is why there is an insistence upon the self. In the love poems the answer might be lust, love or the desire to exert power. Another relevant feature in many of the love poems is the passivity of the mistress. In the religious poems, however, the insistence upon the self arises out of need, and God is usually seen, or asked to be, active – *Divorce me, untie, or break that knot again (Holy sonnet 14* (11)). What might be said to distinguish the religious poems from the love poems is the quality of need; a lover needs a beloved in a narrow sense, but a soul that knows itself to be sinful and lost needs God in the most vital and fundamental way. It is worth asking whether it is egotistical to seek that which is absolutely necessary for one's salvation.

The speaker and the audience

Linked with the issue of egotism is the relationship within the poems between the poet and the one whom he addresses. One of the problems of the love poetry is the question of whether the one who is addressed is *consistently* present throughout the poem. Quite often the reader is aware of her at the start, but as the poem progresses the poet seems to become interested in the convolutions, the twists and turns, of his own thought with the result that the beloved is forgotten. In the love poetry the beloved is often passive, but God is not like a mistress: he is thought of as active. Does this make his presence in the poems more vivid and more consistent? This was certainly the view of one of the leading Donne scholars of this century, Dame Helen Gardner: *His Maker [God] is more powerfully present to the imagination in his divine poems than any mistress is in his love poems*. Try testing out this idea in every poem in this selection.

If this issue of the relationship between the poet and the one whom he addresses is combined with the question of egotism, a way is opened up of thinking about one of Donne's greatest and most enigmatic poems – *A Hymn to God the Father*. The pressure of God is felt in the dark contemplative tone of each line and yet the poet, though desperately unsure of his own salvation, still sports self-indulgently with language even to the extent of a pun on his own name.

The three features of argument, egotism and relationship show that although there are strong continuities between the love and the religious poetry, the world of the religious poetry is, nevertheless, a distinctive one. What else is distinctive about it? Three things are certainly important.

The nature of Donne's religious feeling

The first is the nature of the religious experience that is found in the poems. A reader who is unaccustomed to hearing people use religious language might jump to the conclusion that Donne was an intensely religious man. In one sense such a reader would not be wrong. The poet in the religious poems is someone who is very much aware that he is a sinner who needs the mercy of God. One example is enough to show this: listen to the frank longing of *Yet dearly' I love you, and would be loved fain, Holy sonnet 14* (9) The depth of the need and the anguish of the poet is unusual. But in another sense it is not. The religious experience in these poems is fundamentally that of yearning for an experience of God's mercy, not one of actually receiving it. The poems do not celebrate either moments of conversion when the sinner knows that he or she is saved or moments of spiritual illumination in which the soul establishes a deep, direct and intimate communion with God. Is it true that the poet feels his need much more sharply than he actually feels God? In connection with this, it is again worth thinking about some words of Helen Gardner:

. . . *Donne, though in many other ways a remarkable human being, is not remarkable for any spiritual gifts or graces which we recognize at once as extraordinary and beyond the experience of mankind.*

133

Sin and salvation

It must be said that the range of Donne's religious poetry is narrow. In theological terms the themes are twofold: sin and salvation. Sin is a much misunderstood word. It means far more than committing immoral acts such as stealing or murder. For a start, the word covers intention as well as the act. But far more important than individual acts of immorality is the relationship between sin and God. Sin is always against God, and so the one who sins is alienated, or separated, from God. Moreover, because God is the source of all holiness and goodness, the sinner is condemned in the eyes of God. But sin is not only a matter of deliberate acts; because of the fall of man (the story of Adam and Eve, in *Genesis 2-3*, recounts how mankind fell from favour with God and was consequently expelled from the Garden of Eden) everyone inherits the mark or stain of sin as part of his or her own human nature. This is called original sin. The plight of sinful humanity is so desperate that it cannot save itself; only God can offer mercy, grace and salvation. This God has done in the life, and particularly the death, of Christ. The anguish in Donne's religious poems is an indication of how seriously he regards his own sin and how deep is his need of salvation. The themes may be few, but in the terms of Christian theology they are the central ones.

The preoccupation with salvation or, to use another term, redemption, is evident in the language of the poems. In addition to *sin* and *death* there is *fear* (fear that one may not be saved) and *despair* - the most terrible of religious words because the person who despairs of his or her own salvation is almost inevitably lost. Words concerned with salvation also appear - *repent, delivery, purged, pardon, blood* and *grace*.

One of the features of these poems is that salvation is often viewed in what, in theological terms, is called an eschatological or apocalyptic perspective. 'Eschatology' means the end of the world and 'apocalyptic' means revelation. Taken together they refer to what are called the four last things: death, judgement, heaven and hell. Throughout the middle ages these things were imagined as happening dramatically: world history would end, Christ would return in glory, angels would blow trumpets, the dead and the living would be brought to the judgement seat of Christ, where some would be judged worthy of heaven whilst others would be condemned to hell. The images people used to make this scene vivid were originally drawn from *The Bible*, particularly *1 Corinthians and Revelation* (a book which is concerned with the Last Judgement), and later embroidered and extended by poets, artists and theologians. In most medieval churches a picture, called a doom, of the Last Judgement was painted above the chancel arch. Much of the intensity of Donne's religious poetry is due to his employment of eschatological images. Sometimes he views the scene communally as in the octave of *Holy sonnet 7* and sometimes he sees salvation in starkly personal terms, as in *Holy sonnet 6*. But whether he sees judgement as universal or individual he views it in such a heightened way as to make the reader unsure about his real feelings. Do we just see his fear and dread, or does he also feel a strange thrill at the terrors of Judgement Day?

Paradox

Paradox is a statement which appears to be self-contradictory but which in its clash of opposites reveals a new and very often important truth. Paradox, then, is not just a game played with words; it is a way of expressing central truths. Christian theology has always employed paradoxes. Jesus taught that he who loses his life shall *find* it, and theologians, following this insight, teach that the only way in which people can be *free* is by dedicating themselves wholly to the *service* of God. Perhaps the central Christian paradox is the one that haunted Donne - that in order to truly live we must die.

Activity

Consider how Donne employs paradoxes in *Holy sonnet 14*.

Discussion

> The idea that the only way he can *rise*, and *stand* is to be overthrown
> and the final thought that he can never be *free* until he is enthralled
> (taken prisoner) nor ever *chaste* until ravished (a word very close in
> meaning to rape) can be interpreted as imaginative variations of the
> basic Christian paradox that true life only comes through death. The
> paradoxes of lines 13-14 can be seen as reinforcing the paradox in line
> 3, emphasizing the importance of paradox to the structure of the poem
> as a whole.

Why was Donne so attracted to paradoxes? Apart from their centrality in Christian thinking, can other reasons be found? Certainly the tensions in his verse between body and soul, the self and another person, between love for the world and love for God, between the desire to draw attention to himself and the desire for firmness and restraint, and, running through all the poems, the tension between thought and feeling point to someone for whom experience itself was paradoxical. But another reason can be offered: paradox offers the poet the opportunity of displaying his verbal skill. Was Donne attracted to paradox because it appealed to his love for language that was playful, intricate and intellectually complex?

Donne and his age

The problems of historical study

When an author is studied historically an assumption is made that the age in which he lives has a shaping influence upon his or her thought. The exact nature of this relationship between an author's work and the life that author lived is always difficult to think about. There is, for instance, the very delicate matter of how the author was influenced by the times in which he or she lived, and the accompanying problem of the extent to which an author transformed the ideas absorbed from the prevailing culture - its religion, philosophy and politics. Even more delicate is the business of estimating the extent to which an author was indebted to assumptions that were so basic to that culture that they were rarely or even never stated. A further problem is that an author's life might be very interesting in itself and yet have very little, and certainly no direct, bearing upon his or her work. In view of these problems, Donne's life will be dealt with only in so far as it touches upon the verse, and the culture of the Sixteenth and Seventeenth centuries will be discussed in relation to the poetry he wrote.

Religious change

Basic to Donne's life and age was religious conflict. The religious history of the Sixteenth and Seventeenth centuries is a very complex one, because the motives of those involved were very mixed; the influences, particularly from the Continent, strong yet varying in character, and the religious issues bound up with social, political and economic concerns. In 1532 Henry VIII opened up a breach with the Church of Rome by establishing himself as Supreme Head of the Church in England. This move was political; Henry had no wish to renounce Catholicism as such. Nevertheless, it is unlikely that he would have been able to oppose the head of the Church – the Pope – had there not been in the country a groundswell of opinion in favour of change, even reform. The demands that people were making of the Church were ones of practice rather than of doctrine: they wanted better priests, services they could more easily understand and *The Bible* in English. Once the break with Rome occurred these pressures, which became pressures for reform, resulted in the dissolution, or closure, of the monasteries (they had been accused, sometimes rightly and sometimes wrongly, of corruption) and the gradual removal of the visible signs of Catholicism; statues, screens in churches, wall paintings and some ritual actions and special clothes (vestments) worn in services. The reign of Edward VI saw the publication of *The Prayer Book* in English, and, although under the Catholic Queen Mary Catholicism was restored, the process of reformation continued in the reign of Elizabeth I. The religion that emerged in Elizabeth's England retained much that was Catholic – an emphasis upon the sacraments of baptism and holy communion, the three orders of ministry, Bishops, priests and deacons, and those statements of Christian belief, the Creeds, but it was visually plainer, more verbal (the *Homilies*, sermons setting out the distinctively English emphases in religion, were to be read in all churches) and, a point to be developed later, more individualistic in character. Although it was not protestant in doctrine, it shared many attitudes with the continental Protestantism.

The influences from abroad strengthened some of these characteristics and introduced new ones. Martin Luther (1483-1546) taught that salvation in no way depended upon mankind proving itself worthy of God's grace, nor buying, as it were, credit with God by performing religious duties such as attending church, fasting and going on pilgrimages. Nor could God's favours be secured by praying to saints who, because of their favoured position, would plead with God for sinful humanity. Instead, Luther, from a study of St Paul's Epistles in *The New Testament*, taught that because God was by his very nature righteous, he could freely make righteous all those who trusted, or, to use the theological word, had faith in him. The proof of God's righteousness was found in the cross of Christ; there God freely offered salvation to all who had faith. Salvation, then, was by faith and not by works; and by works Luther meant any way in which people, through performing religious duties, tried to make themselves worthy of God's mercy. One effect of this was to clear away all that got in the way of the direct relationship between sinful man and righteous God. Another even more powerful influence was John Calvin (1509-64). Calvin, a lawyer by training, was a man of clear intellectual vision and a relentless, one might almost say ruthless, logic. Not only did he teach that salvation was only possible as a gift from God but that God, according to *The Bible*, had already chosen those whom he had elected, or decided, to save. From the beginning of time, Calvin taught, God had predestined (the doctrine was called predestination) some to salvation and others to damnation. This idea, like Luther's, emphasized the individual; if you had been elected by God for salvation your religion was likely to be both inward (you knew you were saved) and individualistic (God had saved *you* but had damned others). Consequently, all the outward signs of religion in which Catholicism had expressed itself - holy water, the ritual actions of the Mass, making the sign of the cross, Masses for the dead, honouring the relics of saints - would seem unnecessary and ridiculous; all that you needed was *The Bible* and preaching, both of which confirmed you in your belief that you were saved.

From Catholic to Anglican

In order to appreciate the bearing this has upon Donne it is necessary to know something of his early life. The most important fact is this: Donne was born a Catholic and became a priest in the Church of England. The family into which he was born in London in the early part of 1572 was one that had remained loyal to 'the old religion' - Catholicism. From 1584 he studied at Hart Hall, Oxford (it was not uncommon for boys as young as 12 to live in University halls) and he probably studied later at Cambridge. As a Catholic, however, he was not allowed to take a degree. In 1592 he went to Lincoln's Inn, one of the Inns of Court of London, where young men went to finish their education and where lawyers studied and practised. It is probable that during his early twenties he began to grow discontented with Catholicism, and, although he very probably studied a great deal of theology at this time, there appears to have been a period when he did not align himself with any particular religious group. It is, however, doubtful that he ever abandoned belief in God. In 1597 he was appointed secretary to the Lord Keeper, a high-ranking court official. The religious significance of this is that such an appointment would have been all but impossible had it been known he was still a

Catholic. By 1605 it is clear that he considered himself an Anglican, a member of the Church of England, because he started to engage in religious controversy against the Church in which he was nurtured. In 1610 he published *Pseudo-Martyr*, an attack upon Catholic unwillingness to take an oath imposed by King James I in 1607.

Problems about faithfulness

What bearing does this change of religion have upon the verse? The first point is one raised by the critic John Carey, who says that a reader must be impressed by the presence in the poetry (both love and religious) of a *perpetual worry about fidelity and falseness*. The implication is that someone who has been unfaithful to his religion and who has found that he can change his loyalties might become nervously aware of the capacity of other people to change their minds or appear to be faithful when they are not. In the light of this suggestion we must consider whether or not a note of unease and even anxiety is present in Donne's love and religious poetry. Why, for instance, does a poem as buoyant as *The Anniversary* introduce the word *treason* (26) or a poem as forthright in its faith as *A Hymn to Christ, at the Author's last going into Germany* contain the cry of what sounds like a puzzled and abandoned lover *Alas, thou lov'st not me* (24)? Donne's change of religion, or, as Catholics might call it, apostasy, might not be the full explanation of such unease but it may have fed a tendency in him to expect change and deceit.

Visual imagery in his poetry

A second way in which his change in religion affects his poetry concerns visual imagery. Catholicism can be said to be a poetic religion in that it developed a wide variety of images (both physical and verbal), whereas Protestantism (here the Anglican Church can be included, although, strictly speaking, it is not a Protestant body) is visually sparer and even, in its extreme forms, austere and bleak. It has often been commented that Donne is not a very visual poet. He shows, for instance, very little interest in nature. Again, it is John Carey who makes the telling point that in *Good Friday, 1613. Riding Westward* there is nothing at all about the countryside through which the poet rides. It is, however, interesting to note that, for Donne, the Holy Sonnets are unusually visual. This may be because he is drawing upon his Catholic upbringing. One of the features of Catholic life in Donne's time was the use of techniques of meditation. Books were written about how to pray and how to deepen one's spiritual life, so that the truths of religion could become a living part of one. One of the things these manuals of devotion, or spiritual exercises, stressed was the visualizing to oneself of a biblical or religious scene. The influence of this tradition of spiritual life may be felt in the uncomfortably physical figure of death in *Holy sonnet 6*, the vivid, eschatological panorama in number 7, the harrowing picture of the crucified Christ in 13 and the powerful picture in 14 of the soul labouring to admit God. The matter, however, is not quite so simple. It could also be argued that in the Holy Sonnets there is a very strong sense of the individual soul before the judgement seat of God, and that is a distinctly Protestant notion.

This brings us to the third way in which the tension between Catholicism and Protestantism might be present in the verse.

Donne's imagination: Catholic or Protestant?

Activity

Read *Holy sonnet 7* paying special attention to the contrast between the first eight lines (the octave) and the last six (the sestet).

Discussion

The octave is highly visual and essentially Catholic in its communal imagery, thought and feeling, whereas the rest of the poem (the sestet) seems quite Protestant in its emphasis upon the individual's relationship with God and the way it is visually restrained.

It would appear that there was both a Catholic and a Protestant imagination in Donne. He responded to the intricate arguments and speculations of Catholic theology, and yet in many poems the voice is independent, and the stress is upon the individual nature of experience. In his public life as a clergyman Donne was one of those who in striving to establish a truly English form of religion attempted to strike a balance between the Catholic heritage and the insights of the reformers. In his poetry the relationship is often one of tension rather than balance. For instance, it is not easy to know whether in using Catholic imagery in *The Canonization* and *The Relic* Donne is imaginatively endorsing a Catholic understanding of the world or whether they are trappings through which a distinctively Protestant voice - restless, assertive, discontented with communal beliefs - speaks.

A great visitor of ladies

The culture of Donne's day may be evident in his verse in other ways. One who claimed to remember him at Lincoln's Inn said that Donne was *a great visitor of ladies*. It is difficult to know what to make of this. One who writes love poetry and poetry of seduction may not himself be a lover or seducer. Donne, it is clear, felt that his early life was not all that it should have been, but it is not clear whether he was thinking of casual sexual encounters or the writing of, in some cases, very explicit love poetry. It is not easy, therefore, to judge the status of those lines in the Holy Sonnets where he helps to form the picture of himself as a man who has turned from the pleasures of carnal love to the love of God. In 13 he contrasts his *profane mistresses* with God and in 19 writes that his contrition is as full of changes as his profane love. Given that the poet delights in making a fiction out of his own experience (see *The Funeral* and *The Relic* where he anticipates reactions to his death) it could be that the profane mistresses were real or an imaginative reconstruction of the one relationship we do know about – his courting of Ann More.

Ann More - Ann Donne

Ann More was a member of the household of Elizabeth Wolley, whom the widowed Lord Keeper, Sir Thomas Egerton, married in 1597. Ann was then about 14. At some time after that she and Donne must have fallen in love, and in 1601, when she was still under the legal age to marry without her father's consent, they were married in secret. Her father was angry. Donne was imprisoned and after his release found it impossible to secure another public position. A friend, Francis Wolley, invited them to live in his Surrey house at Pyrford. Donne was without a job, without prospects of one and in debt. It may be that a poem such as *The Canonization* was written in this period; the world of married love was more secure and more attractive than the hostile public world in which, as an intelligent and gifted young man, he had hoped to prosper. Although it may be fictional, it was in the early years of his married life that he was supposed to have written the letter that by punning on his own name revealed his worldly state: *John Donne Ann Donne Undone*. The Donnes moved later to Mitcham where, with a growing family, they lived a hard if not exactly poverty-stricken life. This may well be the period in which some of the Holy Sonnets were written. (One of the problems of dating Donne's poems is that during his life they circulated in manuscript - handwritten copies - among small groups of friends.) Gradually he found employment; he helped Thomas Morton in writing religious controversy and in 1610 he was given a post by Sir Robert Drury, with whom he travelled to the Continent in 1612. (He had earlier seen military service in the Earl of Essex's expedition to the Azores.) Gradually his doubts about ordination faded, and he became a clergyman in 1615. He was a notable preacher: the love of argument, the speculative flights of the intellect, the intricate playing upon the multiple meanings of words that mark his poetry were also evident in his eloquent, complex and subtly intellectual sermons. From 1617 he was Reader in Divinity in Lincoln's Inn and from 1621 Dean of St Paul's Cathedral. Towards the end of his life he became absorbed with death (it is interesting to ask how evident death is in all his work), posing in a burial shroud for his own memorial and preaching in February 1631 a sermon called *Death's Duel*. He died in March 1631 and was buried in St Paul's. His monument survived the fire and may still be seen in the Cathedral.

Changes in the Seventeenth-century world view

One of the constant features of Donne's life is his appetite for intellectual matters. In addition to his profound and wide knowledge of theology he was deeply read in several fields of learning. This desire for and delight in knowledge is evident in the verse. Perhaps the most important feature of his intellectual life is the change in world view that was taking place. The change was a kind of secular counterpart to the religious conflicts discussed above. The term *world view* is not easy to explain; it means an understanding of the world and the attitudes to and judgements about it that accompanied that understanding. It is important to see that this was not a fixed and given thing. If asked, the man in the seventeenth-century street could not have given a neat, full and coherent statement of his 'world view' any more than the man or woman in a twentieth-century street can give an exhaustive view of all he or she understands, believes and values about the world. Nevertheless, some features can be singled out. There was a fundamental change in people's view of astronomy. One of the most influential models of the world throughout the middle ages was that derived from the second-century thinker Ptolemy. Many medieval people accepted his basic picture of the world (geocentric), while at the same time refining and elaborating it. Ptolemy taught that the earth was the centre of the world, and that the sun, moon, planets and all the stars revolved around it in perfect circles. Interwoven into this picture of the world were the insights of Christianity. Thus, it was held that when mankind fell in the Garden of Eden, sin affected the whole world below the moon, but that above it the blight of the fall was unknown, and the planets and stars revolved in their original brightness. Moreover, as the heavenly bodies revolved, the most wonderful and unearthly music was created (the music of the spheres). Humanity, because of the fall, was deaf to it, though the harmonies of music were valued partly as a dim echo of that heavenly sound.

The idea of earthly music echoing the music of the spheres brings in another influence - Platonism. The Greek philosopher Plato had taught that all earthly things are only pale reflections of a real world of ideal forms, which exists over and above the world in unchanging harmony and peace. This beautiful and enticing idea was attractive in that it made sense of the decay and change in the world and the human desire for a real and permanent world beyond the changes and chances of human life. The Platonic impulse is frequently felt in Donne; think, for instance, about *The Undertaking*. Another Greek philosopher, Aristotle, was influential in shaping people's idea of movement. Beyond the moving spheres of the heavens, people imagined the existence of a first mover - the *Primum Mobile* - which was activated by God and gave motion to the entire universe. This idea is present in *Good Friday, 1613. Riding Westward*.

Alchemy

Alchemy was a dominant influence. It is easy to dismiss alchemy as a ridiculous blend of wrong-headed science and obscure philosophical speculations, but it was, in fact, a highly intricate, intellectually complex tradition of thinking about the nature of the world and the relationships between people and the rest of the created order. It was concerned both with experiments and with abstract philosophizing. It worked with a picture of the world in which all matter was based upon four elements: earth, air, fire and water. There was speculation that beyond these observable elements there existed a fifth, the quintessence, the discovery of which would benefit humanity because it would cure all diseases. Another alchemical enterprise was the search for the philosopher's stone, which would be able to change ordinary metals into gold. This idea was again associated with health (gold was thought to be a cure for many diseases) and philosophical ideas that held that gold was the highest of all metals. The changing of metals into gold thus became a symbol of the transformation of base and ordinary things into fine and valuable things.

The new and the old in Donne's poetry

Donne's reading would have made him familiar with ideas about astronomy and alchemy. (You should, of course, remember that these ideas would be known to him in all their intellectual subtlety and not in the rough sketch given above.) But from his reading Donne would also be aware of thought that challenged these ideas. Copernicus (1473-1543) offered a different picture of the world (a heliocentric view); although he held to the idea that planets revolved in circles he claimed that it was the sun and not the earth around which they moved. The emotional effect of this must have been very strong: the earth and those who lived in it were no longer the centre of things. The blow to human pride must have been immense. Elsewhere there were the beginnings of what we now know as modern science; in anatomy, cartography (map-making), medicine, mathematics and physics new discoveries showed the world to be a natural object rather than something which had moral as well as natural properties. Alchemy, too, came in for increasing criticism. The tone of *Love's Alchemy* partly stems from the poet's dismissal of alchemists as ridiculous and misguided.

The influence these intellectual changes had on Donne's poetry may be found in his imagery. Donne draws upon both new and old learning. He touches upon the debate about the nature of angels' understanding (*The Dream*), the state of those in heaven (*The Anniversary*), the nature of the soul (*The Ecstasy*), the earth as the centre of the universe (*The Sun Rising*) and the work of the alchemists (*A Nocturnal upon S. Lucy's Day, being the shortest day*). But he is also aware of the learning that was replacing these ideas: in *The Funeral* he refers to contemporary ideas about how the brain controls the body; in *The Good Morrow* he speaks of sea-discoverers and the art of map-making (map-making also occurs in *Hymn to God my God, in my Sickness*) and in *A Valediction, forbidding Mourning* there is, after images drawn from Ptolemy's astronomy and alchemy, the *stiff twin compasses*, a symbol, possibly, of the new world of exploration. The result gives us a fascinating variety of images, often within one poem. The interesting question is which most appealed to Donne's imagination: is he imaginatively more at home with the harmonious picture of an earth-centred universe, or is he excited by new discoveries?

Donne's language

The Petrarchan tradition

Donne would find more than academic learning in his culture. From his days at Lincoln's Inn as a young man, and almost certainly (though there is no direct evidence) throughout his courtship and early years of marriage to Ann More he wrote love poetry. Nor was love poetry written only in his youth. Scholars who have argued about the date of *A Nocturnal upon S. Lucy's Day, being the shortest day* put it, at its earliest, in 1612, that is, three years after the probable date of some of the Holy Sonnets. It is important to ask what influences a love poet was open to at this period. Although Donne is (rightly) praised for the striking individuality of his verse, particularly its constantly changing rhythms, he is greatly indebted to the traditions of Petrarchan love poetry. Petrarch (1304-74), an Italian poet who wrote love poems addressed to Laura, established a number of conventions as to how lover-poets should speak and present themselves. These can be seen in many of the love poems written throughout the sixteenth century. They can also be seen in Donne: to part from a beloved was death (*The Expiration*); a mistress could be indifferent and cruel (*Twicknam Garden*); the beloved was looked upon as the soul of the world (*The Fever*); love was a religion (*The Canonization, The Relic*); lovers existed in beautiful landscapes (the opening of *The Ecstasy*); lovers performed superhuman tasks for their mistresses (*Song: Go, and catch a falling star*) and insects were envied for the intimacy they enjoyed with the body of the mistress (*The Flea*). But this is not to say that in these and other poems Donne does no more than follow conventions. For instance, the cynical close of *Song: Go, and catch a falling star* is a departure from the Petrarchan conventions with which the poem started, and the sordid realism of *The Apparition* and the dismissive snorts of *Love's Alchemy* are only dependent upon Petrarchan conventions in so far as these conventions are subverted and overthrown. There is, however, more to Donne's originality than his relationship with Petrarchan conventions; other aspects of his poetic language must be considered.

The arresting openings in Donne's poetry

Activity

Think about the impact of the following openings.

I wonder by my troth, what thou, and I
Did, till we loved?   (*The Good Morrow*)
Busy old fool, unruly sun,
Why dost thou thus,
Through windows, and through curtains call on us?
                                        (*The Sun Rising*)

Once, and but once found in thy company,
All thy supposed escapes are laid on me

(Elegy 4)

Discussion

To be a reader of Donne is, in a special sense, to be a listener. In each of the above openings you can hear a distinctive note struck: what I see in the first is delighted discovery, in the second scornful anger, in the third the venting of frustration. What is immediately present to me is an individual voice, someone to whom that voice speaks and a strong sense of the occasion or situation that has impelled the poet to speak. Your opinion may differ. You may, for example, interpret the second opening as humorous rather than scornful.

It is not surprising that Donne the poet has been compared to the dramatists of his own day, who gave characters long speeches in which they presented themselves to other characters and the audience. The openings, however, present a problem: some readers have felt that whilst they are vividly impressive, the dramatic tension is not always sustained. This is something you will have to think about: do the poems flag after their vigorous openings, or is it wrong to expect a poet (or any artist) to sustain the high emotional pressure of an opening? In music, for instance, openings are often different from, and more arresting than, other parts of the work, precisely because it is the purpose of openings to attract, stir and impress.

The dramatic quality

Even though the drama of the openings might not always be sustained, it is possible to talk about the dramatic quality of Donne's verse as a whole. One of the forms he uses is what may be loosely called the 'dramatic monologue'; that is to say, a poem which presents a character addressing either another person or an audience in a specific situation. Such poems are dramatic in so far as readers are aware of the context or plot which has impelled the character to speak, and a monologue because there is one voice and, possibly, the expression, albeit sketchy, of a personality. *The Apparition* and *Woman's Constancy* are usually described as dramatic monologues, and the Elegies share many of their qualities. In other poems the reader is made aware, sometimes vividly so, of the situation out of which the poet speaks: in *The Canonization* he is angry with someone who has tried to criticize his loving; in *The Dream* he has just been awakened by his beloved; in *A Jet Ring Sent* he balances a ring on his finger, and in *Twicknam Garden* he looks about him to find evidence of the Spring. There are also hints of personality or, at the very least, moods: the poet of *The Ecstasy* is both sensitive and possessed of a refined and subtle intellect; and in *The Undertaking* there is the suggestion of pride in what he judges to be his heroic achievement.

Rhythms and cadences

The rhythms of Donne's verse are dramatic, because there is an interplay between the expectation of a regular pattern of stresses and the irregular movement of natural speech. Listen again to the opening of *The Good Morrow*:

> I wonder by my troth, what thou, and I
> Did, till we loved? (1-2)

The first line is regular apart from *what*: that is to say, with the exception of that word, every second syllable is stressed. Why does *what* disturb this pattern? The clue might be that it is the word which focuses the poet's question; I *wonder* expresses an amazement, which is given a precise form by *what*. In natural speech the importance of a word such as *what* is brought out by stress; for instance nowadays we might say: 'And what do you think?' This is what happens in *The Good Morrow*: *what* disturbs the regularity of the live by bringing to it the alien movement of a natural speaking voice. The effect is dramatic.

The rhythmic interplay enforces both the sense of wonder and the pressure of the poet's strenuous enquiry.

But in matters of rhythm there can be no *single* correct performance. (Though there are many wrong ones.) Readers will differ on whether or not to stress a word, the weight of stresses, the number and length of pauses and the relative pace of lines. Such variations in reading underline the fact that to perform (read aloud) a poem is to interpret it. This is why in the Notes you are sometimes asked to think about an issue by practising different readings.

Inseparable from the question of Donne's rhythms are his cadences. A cadence is the movement towards a close (the end of a clause, a line or sentence) of the rhythm and pitch of a set of words. Because the pressures of the speaking voice are present in Donne's poems, each cadence is distinctive. Nevertheless, the mood of each poem is partly established by a series of cadences that have a family resemblance. There is, however, a cadence which is characteristically Donne's and which is present in a number of his poems - the cadence that rises to form a triumphant conclusion.

Activity

Think about the character of the final cadence in these lines from the close of the first verse of *The Anniversary*.

    Only our love hath no decay;
This, no tomorrow hath, nor yesterday,
Running it never runs from us away,
But truly keeps his first, last, everlasting day.

                                        (7-10)

Discussion

After cadences that are assured and steady the last line winds up, so to speak, with the words *first*, *last* – the beginning and the end of time – and then completes the sweeping upward movement as the voice pronounces the crucial and climactic *everlasting*, a word which shifts the thought of the line from time into eternity.

The rhythms of speech counterpointing regular metre and the

contribution of cadence are two of the 'physical' or 'material' elements ('physical' and 'material' because they appeal directly to the senses) that make Donne's language distinctive. There are others: you should think about the variation in line length, the effect of short lines and the impact of rhyme. Also of importance is his use of monosyllables. Although the English language has a high proportion of words of one syllable, it is still rare to find whole lines which are entirely monosyllabic. When they occur in Donne, the effect can often be of someone pondering intently weighty and even urgent matters. Listen to the way the poet of *A Hymn to God the Father* spells out clearly to himself the desperate state he fears he may be in, and how the deliberate monosyllables act as a foil, and thereby emphasize the most frightening word of all, the word of damnation – *perish*:

> I have a sin of fear, that when I have spun
>   My last thread, I shall perish on the shore   (13-14)

When considering the 'physical' and 'material' aspects of his language it is important to do more than merely recognize them as interesting rhythms and cadences. They matter because they contribute to the variety of mood and movement in a Donne poem. *Mood* and *movement* are, in a sense, misleading; what must be stressed is that the mood emerges in and through the movement of the lines, and that the movement of the lines is the effect of the poet's changing moods. To read a Donne poem is to be conscious of a self in a constant state of emotional and intellectual flux. This may be why the critic F. R. Leavis said that we read Donne *as we read the living* – in the rhythms, cadences and physical textures of his verse a reader can sense the constantly-changing moods, impulses and ideas which are the defining characteristics of a living self. Another way of putting the point is to say that Donne's poetry not only conveys ideas and feelings but the actual living experience of what it is like to think and feel.

Activity

Think about the intellectual and emotional pulse of these lines from *The Flea*.

Oh stay, three lives in one flea spare,
Where we almost, nay more than married are. (10-11)

Discussion

In trying to stop his mistress from killing the flea he asserts what he is quite certain of – the *three lives* in the *one flea*. The line obliges a performer to lay particular stress on *three* and *one*, and it is also worth asking whether *lives* too should bear an equal emphasis. He then becomes speculative and perhaps a little tentative; one can hear him turning over the possibilities in the way in which almost bears a lingering and a heavy stress on the first syllable and is slightly separated from the two preceding words. The even longer caesura (pause) after *almost* acts out the moment when an even more compelling thought occurs to him. The interjection *nay* is the act in which he possesses with certainty the idea that what happens in the flea is (note the heavy stress of a decisive voice) *more* than a marriage. What is given in those five lines, then, is not just thought but the experience of what it is like to feel one's way through thoughts.

The love of argument

One of the things that the rhythms and cadences of Donne's thought make clear is a delight in thinking and argument. Donne (or the poets in the poems) seizes quickly the opportunity to launch an argument or sport his learning, with the result that the pace of thinking is often rapid and, occasionally, the arguments compressed. Sometimes the argument is not easily understood upon a first reading; what is usually clear, however, is the relish with which it is pursued. There is an audible delight in the precision of:

It were but madness now t' impart
    The skill of specular stone,
When he which can have learned the art
    To cut it, can find none.   *The Undertaking* (5-8)

The purposeful movement of the verse to the firm stress on *cut* is not just a progression towards a conclusion but an expression of the deft skill of the poet who has neatly cut, or clinched, his argument. Delight in this precision of execution is often present in the words which, so to speak, scaffold the argument: it is always worthwhile attending to Donne's use of such apparently insignificant words as *so, if, but, then* and the phrases which qualify his statements – *which is, as I have, if they do* (all from *The Undertaking*).

The wrong key

Donne's pronounced pleasure in argument raises two problems. The poet John Dryden expressed one very forcefully when he said that Donne *perplexes the minds of the fair sex with nice speculations of philosophy, when he should engage their hearts, and entertain them with the softness of love.* The thrust of Dryden's remark is to question whether Donne's poetry is, so to speak, in the wrong key. Is he too interested in spelling out an argument and too unconcerned about how his beloved will respond? At least two replies are possible: it could, for instance, be said that part of Donne's courtship is a desire to entertain his beloved with a wild and intricate argument in the hope that she will be delighted at the playful reasoning and amused by the absurdities of its exaggerations. A second possible defence is that the arguments control the emotions of the poet, and that, therefore, in each piece of reasoning there is the subdued pressure of feeling.

Reason and emotion

The difficulty of Donne's verse touches on the second issue: the relationship in the poem between reason and emotion. The movements of Donne's poetry are expressive of thoughts and feelings; the question is how those two things are connected. In this century the emphasis has been upon the fusion of thought and feeling; Donne has been praised because his verse uniquely combines the two so that there is emotion in the thought, and the feeling is intimately related to the business of thinking. The poet T. S. Eliot made this point so persuasively in 1921 that critics have repeated it ever since. Writing of Chapman, a sixteenth-century poet, he says:

. . . there is a direct sensuous apprehension of thought or a re-creation of thought into feeling, which is exactly what we find in Donne.

Eliot's language makes the point: Donne, he states, not only apprehends thought, he does so through the senses – *direct sensuous* – so that the experience of thinking is also an emotional one. Is this true? Is the thought always felt or recreated into feeling? Read the verse with the possibility in mind that in Donne there is this remarkable fusion of thought and feeling and then ask whether it has been achieved. In *A Fever* the poet starts anxiously:

Oh do not die, for I shall hate
All women so, when thou art gone,
That thee I shall not celebrate,
When I remember, thou wast one.   (1-4)

There is a good case for saying that the thought the poetry celebrates is recreated, and made personal, by the poet's concern for his beloved. But can the same be said of the second verse?

But yet thou canst not die, I know
  To leave this world behind, is death.
But when thou from this world wilt go,
  The whole world vapours with thy breath.   (5-8)

Do you feel the pressure behind these words of his anxiety, or do you just hear an argument deftly executed?

Activity

Is there a change in the first verse of *Song: Sweetest love* from thought which is inseparably fused with loving concern for the beloved to a purely intellectual interest in the idea of practising dying?

> Sweetest love, I do not go,
>   For weariness of thee,
> Nor in hope the world can show
>   A fitter love for me;
>   But since that I
> Must die at last, 'tis best
> To use myself in jest
>   Thus by feigned deaths to die.   (1-8)

Discussion

You might agree that there is a shift after line 4 from feeling and thought fused to thought alone. Alternatively, you might decide that there is a shift but it is from one blend of thought and feeling - a desire to share reasons with her - to a different idea - the delight in a new idea.

The fusion of thought and feeling has often been seen as one of the highest achievements of art, and it is understandable that readers have wanted to find it in Donne. It remains, however, something that you will have to test out for yourself. But on occasions it seems to me that its presence is unmistakable. In the last stanza of *Song: Sweetest love* the poet says:

> Let not thy divining heart
>   Forethink me any ill   (33-34)

Here the heart which is the seat of feeling is divining (foreseeing) and can *forethink*: the very subject is how feeling and thought feed on each other, and the gentle rhythm which leads to a strong stress on *forethink* acts out the experience of emotion generating thought.

Language as a subject

The fact that the fusion of thought and feeling becomes the subject of the verse leads naturally into one of the most interesting features of Donne's work. In his poetry language – speech, thought, expression – actually becomes one of his subjects. Part of the triumph of loving is saying what one has done:

> If, as I have, you also do
>   Virtue attired in woman see,
> And dare love that, and say so too
>
> *(The Undertaking)*

But language can break down:

>   but now alas,
> All measure, and all language, I should pass,
> Should I tell what a miracle she was.   *(The Relic)*

These are not isolated examples: *The Apparition* turns on *what I will say;* the poet of *Love's Alchemy* reviews his past in these terms *I have loved, and got, and told; The Canonization* begins with the poet telling the interfering onlooker *hold your tongue* and ends with an intention *to build in sonnets pretty rooms;* in *The Ecstasy* the body is his (the soul's) book and *Hymn to God my God, in my Sickness* ends with the poet preaching to himself *Be this my text, my sermon to mine own.*

Metaphysical poetry

It is perhaps not surprising that poetry which is so aware of language should have stimulated literary critics to develop a specialized vocabulary to talk about it. Donne is said to be a metaphysical poet. Metaphysics is that branch of philosophy which deals with any matter beyond what can be located through the senses; thus time (you can not see time, only its effects), the mind, free will and God are subjects of metaphysical thought. The term was originally applied to Donne because of his use of academic learning. It is also applicable in that many of his subjects are metaphysical in themselves; for instance, the relationship between souls is the subject of *The Ecstasy*. Yet if you want to handle the term you must exercise care. Helen Gardner, for instance, has pointed out that Donne is a moral rather than a metaphysical poet because he explores meta-physical ideas *not for their own sake, but for the light they throw on his true subject, the heart of man*. It is important to think about whether that is true. Is he interested in the truth or falsity of the ideas he employs or does he use them as figures of speech to throw light upon human attitudes and emotions?

In practice, the term metaphysical is used more broadly than this discussion has indicated. Donne is said to be metaphysical because, like some other seventeenth-century poets, such as Herbert and Crashaw, his verse displays certain characteristics, only a few of which are related to metaphysical thinking as such. Thus Donne is a metaphysical poet because his verse is characterized by arresting openings, intricate arguments, para-doxes, hyperbole (exaggeration), analogies drawn from differ-ent branches of learning, plays upon the rich potential of meaning in individual words, tensions between regular metre and the natural rhythms of speech, sudden outbursts of passion, an obsessive interest in mortality and, sometimes, a world-weary cynicism.

Wit

Donne's poetry was not called metaphysical till after Dryden had commented in the late seventeenth century that he *affects the metaphysics*. The word that was widely used in Donne's own day to characterize his use of language was wit. Wit primarily meant the expression of a lively intelligence; it was seen in the quickness of the mind, its ability to see connections and in the skill with which words were handled so as to bring out their levels of meaning. Donne makes wit one of his subjects in *A Fever*:

> Oh wrangling schools, that search what fire
>   Shall burn this world, had none the wit
> Unto this knowledge to aspire,
>   That this her fever might be it? (13-16)

Wit is not only one of the subjects; it is evident in the deft precision of the language. The quickness of the poet's understanding, that her fever is the fire that shall burn at the end of time, is an example of wit, and so is the way he plays upon *fire* and *burn* to bring out their appropriateness to both flames and disease.

The conceit

The term that is used most in discussing Donne is *conceit*. A conceit, like a simile, metaphor or analogy, establishes a relationship between two different things, but what distinguishes a conceit is the remoteness of the objects; that is to say, in a conceit it is the strangeness, even the outrageousness, of the comparison that is important. Furthermore, a conceit is often elaborate and extended in that the strange similarity of the two things is worked out, from line to line, in considerable detail. The effect of the conceit is that a reader is usually surprised at the oddity, even absurdity, of the comparison, but as it unfolds its appropriateness becomes clear.

Activity

Think about how the conceit of the marriage temple (church) works in these lines from *The Flea*.

> This flea is you and I, and this
> Our marriage bed, and marriage temple is;
> Though parents grudge, and you, we'are met,
> And cloistered in these living walls of jet. (12-15)

Discussion

> It does seem odd to compare a flea to a church, but the lines unfold the strange reasoning: since it was believed that in sexual intercourse blood was mingled, the flea can be said to be their marriage bed, and since intercourse completes a marriage the flea can also be said to be the place where the marriage is celebrated - a church. If then they are married, neither parents nor the girl can object to intercourse; after all, their state is a holy one because they have become part of the church itself - *cloistered in these living walls of jet.*

Two very interesting problems are raised by conceits. The first is whether their significance is local or whether they extend to the poem as a whole. Should a reader, for instance, see the conceit as illuminating the area of the poem in which it occurs, or, to continue using the metaphor, does it shed light on the whole poem? This is not something that can be decided by a general rule; each poem must be thought about. In the case of each conceit you might ask: how far can its significance be pushed? In the case of *The Flea* it is worth asking whether the conceit of the marriage temple is basic to the poem, pointing as it does, to the poet's desire to make love to his mistress and his persuasion that there is nothing improper in this. In the case of *The Canonization* there is a conceit in which the lovers' sexual vitality is presented in the conceit of the phoenix riddle. Does this elaborate play upon the sexual meaning of dying and rising extend to other areas of the poem or is its significance confined to the stanza in which it appears?

The other problem is their intellectual status; that is to say, do they just help to illuminate human experience, or do they also show what the world is actually like? This issue is very much affected by the intellectual fashions of literary criticism; at some periods, critics like to see literature as a mirror of the world, at others they want to locate truth in psychological terms and so see claims about reality as actually being about the human mind or heart, and then on other occasions the fashion is to see literature as being about the resources of language and not about the world outside or the human world within. You may find that how you view the world will affect your reading of Donne and, of course, other writers. The best approach to the issue of intellectual status is to ask of every poem, or, more particularly, every conceit: do I find this strange yet true or do I merely find it strange? That question is very dependent upon Dr Johnson's remarks in his *Life of Cowley* on the metaphysical style. He said that in metaphysical poets their *thoughts are often new, but seldom natural* and that in their poems the *most heterogeneous ideas are yoked by violence together*. Johnson clearly sides with those who find Donne's language strange but not true. You may feel that this is the case. It is also possible to find that his unusual language expresses the tensions of human feeling and that his intellectual ingenuity serves to show our richly complex yet unified world in which even apparently unrelated things such as a flea and marriage temples are related.

Conclusion

One of the aims of the *Approaches* has been to introduce you to a number of ways in which Donne can be studied. For instance, in Donne and love the question was asked as to whether male and female readers might respond differently to some of the poems. The assumption behind that question is that being a man or a woman might significantly affect an interpretation, because men and women often value different aspects of a relationship. Assumptions were also present in *Donne and his age*. It was assumed that the religious crisis was central, and, on a more general level, that intellectual fashions exert, so to speak, a pressure upon a writer. Whenever you study a literary work you make assumptions and take up points of view. No critical thinking is without assumptions; it always starts from one viewpoint or another. You should always remember this when you are thinking about Donne. If, for instance, you find one approach unfruitful, look at the poems another way. You may not find it particularly helpful to approach one poem by thinking about the kind of love expressed in it so consider instead the relationship of the poet to the reader, or the relationship of the poet to the person he addresses. You then might think about the argument, the emotional contours of the verse or the way the poem opens and closes. Those are just examples. The important point is that you should always be prepared to select a number of critical viewpoints.

You must, however, remember that critical viewpoints are not a set of keys. A poem is not a very complicated kind of lock which will only yield up the treasures that lie beyond when a certain number of keys are inserted. This is to think of a poem as a set of problems waiting to be solved. This temptation is particularly strong in the case of Donne because he can be so intellectually and emotionally puzzling. A response of many students is to sort out the argument into clear stages and simplify the emotional tensions. It would be a mistake to regard the *Approaches* as a means to that end. It might, for instance, be helpful to remember that Donne was a Catholic who became an Anglican, but that cannot be used to explain away all that seems odd, strange and even mysterious in Donne. One important reason for this is that no matter how much is known about Donne, the poetry remains arrestingly challenging. Of course it is important to know the background to the poems, and of course it is helpful to know whether some words have changed in meaning (both *Approaches* and the *Notes* should be a help here), but neither knowledge of background nor a familiarity with crucial words can help you to say what it is about Donne that is so arresting and challenging. There is an untarnished strangeness about the thought and feeling in the poetry of Donne, and no study could or should seek to cloud it. Studying Donne is not a question of being so familiar with his work that poems cease to puzzle but of learning to live with problems so that you enjoy their bracing company.

Chronology of Donne's life and times

Events in Donne's life

1572 Born in London into a Catholic family.

1576 Death of father.

1584 Starts his education at Oxford. Because he was Catholic, he was not allowed to take a degree.

1588-9 It is possible that he studies at Cambridge.

1591 Begins law studies in London. Reads widely in Theology and possibly writes some of the *Songs and Sonnets*.

1593 His brother, Henry, is imprisoned for hiding a Catholic priest in his house. He dies in Newgate prison.

1596 Takes part in the expedition to Cadiz (Spain) when it is taken and looted.

1597 Sails on the 'Islands' expedition. Later he is a member of an expedition to the Azores. On his return he becomes secretary to the Lord Keeper, Sir Thomas Egerton.

Historical events

1576 Building of the first theatre in London.

1577-80 Drake circumnavigates the world.

1587 Execution of the Catholic Mary Queen of Scots.

1588 The Spanish Armada is defeated. One of its aims was toleration for English Catholics. Probable date of Shakespeare's first play, *The Comedy of Errors*.

1591 Publication of Sir Philip Sidney's *Astrophel and Stella*, a sonnet sequence written according to Petrarchan conventions.

1595 Sir Walter Ralegh's voyage to Guiana.

1599 The Globe Theatre is opened by Shakespeare's company of players.

Events in Donne's life

1601 Becomes an MP but takes no part in debates or committees. Secretly marries Ann More, then under 21.

1605 Travels on the Continent. Visits Paris and may have visited Venice. Returns in 1606.

1606 Moves with his growing family to Mitcham, Surrey.

1607 Takes lodgings in the Strand while seeking a public office.

Establishes a firm friendship with Lucy, Countess of Bedford, who moves into Twickenham Park. *Twickenham Garden* may date from this period. It is probable that most of the *Holy Sonnets* were written between 1607 and 1611.

Bishop Morton urges him to be ordained as a priest. He declines. He probably assists Morton in religious controversies, arising from the Gunpowder plot.

1609 *The Expiration* is published in Ferrabosco's *Airs*.

Historical events

1600 The East India Company is formed. Essex rebellion against Elizabeth I fails.

1600–1 Probable date of Shakespeare's *Hamlet*.

1602 Imprisoned for the secret marriage, dismissed by Sir Thomas Egerton, and, when released, lives in Pyrford, Surrey. *The Sun Rising* and *The Canonization* may date from this period.

1603 Death of Elizabeth I. James I becomes King.

1603–4 Plague is very severe in London.

1605 The Gunpowder Plot fails As a result the loyalty of Catholics to the State becomes a controversial issue.

1609 Publication of Kepler's work confirms that the earth revolves around the sun.

1610	*Pseudo-Martyr*, a work of religious controversy directed against Catholics, is published. Donne is awarded an honorary Master of Arts (MA) by Oxford University.
1611	He travels with Sir Robert Drury on the Continent, staying at Amiens and Paris. His departure may have prompted him to write *Song: Sweetest love* and *Valediction: forbidding Mourning*. When he returns in 1612 he lodges in Drury House, Drury Lane, when he remains till 1621.
1614	Sits in Parliament, serving on four committees.
1615	Ordained priest. Becomes a royal chaplain and receives a Doctor of Divinity (DD) from Cambridge University.
1616	Preaches at Court. Becomes Reader in Divinity at Lincoln's Inn.
1617	Preaches at Paul's Cross, a famous pulpit in the grounds of St Paul's Cathedral.
	His wife dies after giving birth to a stillborn child. She was 33 and had borne 12 children, 7 of which survived her.
1619	Appointed chaplain to Lord Doncaster's embassy to Germany. Writes *Hymns to Christ*. Visits Heidelberg, where he preaches. Return in 1620.

1610	Galileo's *Sidereus Nuncias* again confirms that the sun is the centre of the solar system.
1611	Publication of the Authorised Version of the *Bible*.
1616	Death of William Shakespeare.

Events in Donne's life

1620 A portrait painted.
1621 Elected Dean of St Paul's Cathedral and preaches there on Christmas Day.
1622 Resigns as reader in Divinity at Lincoln's Inn. Two sermons are published.
1623 Seriously ill; probably writes *Hymn to God my God, in my Sickness* and *A Hymn to God the Father*.
1625 Preaches at court to Charles I.
1628 Ill from August to October.
1630 Makes his will.
1631 Dies and is buried in St Paul's.
1632 Memorial statue erected in St Paul's.
1633 First *Collected Poems* published.

Historical events

1625 Death of James I, Charles I becomes king.
1628 William Harvey's *De Motu Cordis* establishes the theory of the circulation of blood.

Further Reading

There are many books about John Donne and his work. The following may be useful.

John Carey: *John Donne: Life, Mind and Art* (Faber and Faber, 1990). The book is full of ideas and insights into poetry. An unusual aspect is the way the author tries to integrate critical commentary and biographical details.

J. B. Leishman: *The Monarch of Wit* (Hutchinson, 1951). This is a full-length study of Donne which tries to do justice to literary as well as historical problems.

Wilbur Sanders: *John Donne's Poetry* (Cambridge, 1971). A robust yet sensitive reading of the verse which includes lengthy examinations of several of the major poems.

A useful collection of critical essays can be found in *The Metaphysical Poets*, edited by Gerald Hammond (Casebook series, Macmillan, 1974). It contains the important essay by T. S. Eliot and an interesting article by S. L. Bethel on 'The Nature of Metaphysical Wit'.

Also very useful is another collection: *Seventeenth Century English Poetry*, edited by William R. Keast (Galaxy, 1962). This contains F. R. Leavis's important piece 'The Line of Wit', Dame Helen Gardner's essay 'The Metaphysical Poets' and the controversy between C. S. Lewis and Joan Bennet on the nature of Donne's love poetry.

The most important historical essay is Samuel Johnson's 'The life of Cowley'. It is sometimes printed separately, but originally is the first essay in his *Lives of the English Poets*.

There are two good paperback editions of the poetry, both of which have notes on allusions and paraphrases of difficult lines. They are: *John Donne: The Complete English Poems*, edited by A. J. Smith (Penguin, 1971). *The Complete English Poems of John Donne*, edited by C. A. Patrides (Everyman, 1985).

The best biography is R. C. Bald: *John Donne: A Life* (Oxford, 1970).

Tasks

1   Read *The Canonization*, *The Damp*, *The Good Morrow* and *The Sun Rising*. In all these poems there is a (sometimes frank) recognition of the physical aspects of love. Does Donne successfully do justice to the physical side of love as just one of the elements in loving, or does a preoccupation with physical love narrow the range of the poems and diminish the range of meanings in the word 'love'?

2   Consider the roles of men and women in the following poems in the light of the discussion in Approaches pp.120-7: *Elegy 16*, *The Damp*, *The Sun Rising* and *The Funeral*.

3   Compare Donne's treatment of love in *The Flea* with his treatment of love in *The Good Morrow*.

4   Some readers think Donne is obsessed with the dark side of loving - it's resentments, unsatisfied lusts, and pains of parting - whilst others have found him to be the poet of triumphant love. Which voice do you think is the more prominent?

5   Try to put down in writing exactly what the religious poems share with the love poems and the ways in whch they are significantly different. You may wish to think about the use of argument in both sets of poems, and the similarities or differences between the relationship of the poet with his beloved and that of the poet with God.

6   Consider the view that God is more vividly and consistently present in Donne's religious verse than the beloved is in the love poetry. You may like to consider: *Holy sonnet 14*, *Hymn to God the Father*, *The Flea*, *A Valediction: forbidding Mourning*.

7   Does Donne use paradox in his religious poems to express the mysteries of religious belief and the tensions in himself, or is there a tendency in his work to playfully enjoy the paradoxical possibilities of language as an end in itself? *A Hymn to Christ at the Author's last going into Germany* and *Hymn to God my God, in my Sickness* may be useful when considering this issue.

8   Examine the rhythms and cadences of Donne's poems in order
    to see how they build the impression of someone thinking and
    feeling his way through an important experience. You should
    pay special attention to the way in which the rhythms of
    speech counterpoint the regular stress patterns of his lines.

9   Read *A Valediction: forbidding Mourning, Holy sonnet 10* and
    Holy sonnet 19 in the light of the debate (pp. 125-6) on whether
    Donne blends thought and feeling or whether in his verse the
    two often part company.

10 What qualities do the poems in your selection of Donne's verse
    have in common to justify calling them metaphysical?

11 If you were asked to show the variety of Donne's work, which
    four poems would you choose and why?

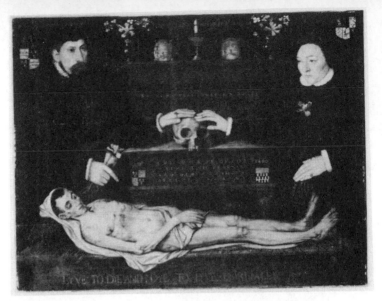

The Judd Memorial.
Pictures that reminded people of
the inevitability of death were
common in Donne's day

A painting of Lucy, Countess
of Bedford by Isaac Oliver. She
lived in Twickenham Park. *Twicknam
Garden* and *A Nocturnal Upon S. Lucy's Day* may be connected with her

Corporis hæc Animæ fit Syndon Syndon Jesu
Amen.

John Donne in a shroud. This engraving appeared in *Death's Duel*, a sermon of Donne's published in 1632

Two emblems from Henry Peacham's *Minerva Britanna*,
the top one showing compasses

An unknown youth by Nicholas Hilliard. The youthful love-sick man is reminiscent of a Petrarchan lover

Index of Titles and First Lines